HOW TO BE A MINISTER'S WIFE AND LOVE IT

"Life in a Goldfish Bowl"

by
ALICE TAYLOR

Foreword by Helen Smith Shoemaker

ZONDERVAN
PUBLISHING HOUSE

OF THE ZONDERVAN CORPORATION | GRAND RAPIDS, MICHIGAN 49506

To

GEORGE A. TAYLOR

*the saintly man
who, many years ago,
decided to make me
a preacher's wife*

Without the inspiration of
HELEN S. SHOEMAKER
*and the wise guidance
and kindly counsel of*
FELIX MORLEY
*and the
enthusiastic encouragement of*
WALTER RUSSELL BOWIE
*these words would never
have been written*

HOW TO BE A MINISTER'S WIFE AND LOVE IT
Copyright © 1968 by Zondervan Publishing House
Grand Rapids, Michigan

Library of Congress Catalog Card Number: 68-12956

ISBN 0-310-33131-5

Printed in the United States of America

84 85 86 87 88 — 20 19

CONTENTS

This splendid book for clergy wives hardly needs an introduction. Mrs. Taylor has been an eminently successful clergy wife, both in large city parishes and in a small flourishing country parish.

She has many words of wisdom for us as to the proper relationship, not only toward the minister, who is also a husband, but toward the parishioners whom we serve.

She is a distinguished person in her own right, having served successfully as President of the women of the Protestant Episcopal Diocese of Albany, while her husband was rector of St. Paul's Church in the city of Albany.

During her husband's rectorship at St. David's Church, Baltimore, Maryland, she brought into being numerous small prayer study groups, which she describes in one of the best chapters of the book.

Mrs. Taylor represents in her own person, the type of minister's wife we should all be — one who not only tactfully and wholeheartedly supports her husband in his ministry without usurping in any way his function, but one who also complements him by daring to stir up the gifts that are in her. As a result, God has been able to use her as a creative channel of His love and His power in the lives of innumerable people and as the means of bringing into being a prayer group work which has helped all the women of the church through her widely read pamphlet, *Starting the Prayer Group*. She is capable, executive, dedicated, humble, self-effacing and gifted. Would that we were all as committed to the high vocation to which we clergy wives have been called.

The readers of this book will not only find it delightful and amusing, but challenging and inspiring.

— HELEN SMITH SHOEMAKER

INTRODUCTION

The young bride or wife of a seminary student, about to embark upon her career as clergyman's wife, filled with enthusiasm though tempered with apprehension, wonders to herself, "How will I do?" The minister's wife, in the midstream of life, stands aside for a moment and ponders, "How am I doing?" And the older minister's wife, who can see on the horizon the end of the journey, wonders "How have I done?" It is to these women that this little book mainly addresses itself.

It is hoped, also, that many of the lay people might care to listen in. What goes on in the heart and mind of the wife of your minister? What is she really like? What makes her "tick"?

So much is expected of her — the health of an Amazon and the dedication of a Florence Nightingale, the patience of a Job and the zeal of a Carrie Nation, the peace-loving thoughts of a Ghandi and the fighting spirit of a warrior, the charm of a debutante and the intelligence of a Phi Beta Kappa. Besides this, she must live her life in a goldfish bowl, well aware that it is her sole responsibility to see that the goldfish behave.

Though surrounded with all sorts and conditions of humanity, she is, nonetheless, at times lonely. She does not ask to be excused from her imperfections. She asks only that she be understood.

ALICE J. TAYLOR

NOTE: Though one can easily detect that this has been written by an Episcopalian, such terminology as rector and rectory may be readily changed to pastor, manse or parsonage.

* * * * *1* * * * *

She Wears a Coat of Many Colors

Who is this woman that lives in the rectory? What is her background? Her training? What is she like? Is she so very different from her sisters? Should she be pitied? Or envied? Does she realize she can make or break that man of God with whom she has cast her lot? What is expected of her?

What is she? First and foremost, she must always be herself. Across the years she will have dreams, goals, tensions, failures and temptations, but she must somehow work out her own destiny — never losing her own personality, nor her own identity.

What is her background? She comes from all walks of life, perhaps a nurse, a teacher, a secretary. One of the finest minister's wives I know was a former model. She may come from the farm, the city, the suburbs, or from a foreign land. She may have worked hard or she may have been a social butterfly. Possibly she was brought up in the church or perhaps in a secular non-church-going family. She may have gone to college, maybe not. Although there are some who have been privileged to go through Seminary with their husbands, the majority come to this new life totally unprepared and professionally untrained. She must work for her degree of PW (preacher's wife) at the University of Experience. The woman who can project herself into her career, give herself wholeheartedly, yet somehow remain herself will graduate *cum laude*.

What is she like, this preacher's wife? She will come to this new life with many diverse interests and talents. It may be art, music, gardening, decorating. These should surely be encouraged, not only for the dimensions that it will give to her life, but because this talent may be used to the glory of God. One large church in a suburban parish is blessed with beautiful altar linens and vestments, complete with embroidered emblems and goldwork. This is because a former rector's wife turned her talents and love and time to this handiwork, and has left a never-to-be-forgotten heritage.

Should this woman who lives in the rectory be pitied? Never. Envied? Yes, for there is no life more rewarding. She may travel the world over and there will always be a certain respect for "the cloth." When she goes into a new community, potential friends eagerly await her. She lives in a home in which, in most cases, the church people take great pride; and as a little boy once said to my young son, "Boy, you live in this great big house and it's all for free!"

But no one will say it is an easy life, no matter how rewarding. Even though she must at all times remain herself, the preacher's wife must also grow and mature, adjusting herself to each new turn in the road. A great deal will be expected of her; she will not please the whole congregation, nor should she. Very early in her career, it will be evident that her life cannot be fulfilled alone. She must look to her

Saviour for guidance and help, through prayer and total commitment to God.

In many ways she is a paradox, wearing a coat of many colors. On a notoriously low salary, she must be reasonably well groomed and attractive — well dressed enough to be at home with the woman who buys her clothes at Bergdorf Goodman, yet not so decked out that she is alien to the girl whose wardrobe came from the Nearly New Shop.

She must be able to carry on a conversation with a prominent dignitary, should she be placed next to him at a gala dinner, yet she must be familiar with the small talk of the neighborhood. Although she may be very shy, duty demands that she be outgoing and friendly.

She must be willing to take responsibility, but not so much as to seem bossy; she must be fun-loving, but only to a degree. She should enter into this new life in deep humility, the more so since her husband, in most cases, will be a humble man, who has learned to rely upon God. Any clergyman's wife who begins her career cocksure, with a knowledge of all the answers, heads for disaster.

The Bishop of Malaya, Bishop Koh, has made a strong case for the married clergyman. He insists that his seminary students be married. What a change *this* is from the policies of our seminaries only twenty years ago.

In one of our large northern states, a Diocese was seeking a new Bishop. Several of the clergy had been called together to suggest names to be placed in nomination. After much discussion, one of the clergy made this observation:

"Gentlemen, I find it interesting that one man on our list may be elected partly because of his wife, while another man can *not* be considered mainly because of his wife."

Lord, we pray Thee that Thou wilt be with us and keep us as we enter upon this new undertaking. Let no change or chance take us out of Thy hand; prosper us in our way, and give us grace always to do the things that will please Thee. Amen.**

* Forward Movement: *Prayers for All Occasions*

2

For Better or Worse

"I, George, take thee Alice, to my wedded wife, to have and to hold from this day forward, for better for worse, for richer for poorer, in sickness and in health, to love and to cherish, till death us do part, according to God's holy ordinance; and thereto I plight thee my troth." (*Book of Common Prayer*)

"I, Alice, take thee George, to my wedded husband, to have and to hold from this day forward, for better for worse, for richer for poorer, in sickness and in health, to love and to cherish till death us do part, according to God's holy ordinance; and thereto I give thee my troth." (*Book of Common Prayer*)

The parson is taking unto himself a wife. He will hear these vows uttered many times at God's altar before his ministry comes to a close, but none will have more meaning than his own vows. From this moment, the single parson becomes a team. Ahead lie sorrows and joys, poverty and riches, frustrations and satisfactions, illness and health, but these will be shared together, for "Those whom God hath joined together let no man put asunder." *

For the groom it is his sacred marriage vow, but for the bride it is in a sense, her ordination vow as well. At this moment she is not only committing her whole self to this man whom she has chosen for her life's mate, but she is offering herself totally and unequivocally to Almighty God and to the furtherance of His Kingdom. Small wonder that this step should not be taken "unadvisedly or lightly, but reverently, discreetly, advisedly, soberly, and in the fear of God." * *

From the very beginning, they must acknowledge to themselves and to each other that a certain time must be set aside each day for prayer together. The family that prays together will indeed stay together, for without God's help they will accomplish little. For most couples this might logically be at the end of the day. Of course they will each have their own private devotions, but this is important, this praying together as a man and his wife. Countless books of meditations and helps are available or perhaps thanksgivings and prayers in a more informal manner are preferable. Even the recitation of the Lord's Prayer together will tighten the bonds. But whatever, however, or wherever the prayers, the essential factor is a regular daily habit — a sacred one that must not be broken.

Unlike most marriages there will be a unique factor to this team. *There is only one captain.* No matter how talented or capable the minister's wife, she must always remember that she is not No. 1. A very fine, but rather egotistical clergyman once said to me, about his new bride, "I told her

* *Book of Common Prayer*
* * Forward Movement: *Prayers for All Occasions*

that she would have to be content to be the tail of the kite!" This is putting it a little more bluntly than necessary, but he had the right idea.

It goes without saying that all parochial decisions must be made by the clergyman himself. I am frequently asked such questions as "Don't you think we should have four vases on the altar instead of two?" or "Don't you think our new curate should speak louder?" To these I have a set reply, "You'll have to speak to the rector — that's his department. He runs the church, I run the rectory." For all time she must be willing and proud to accept second billing on the team.

He must be given complete freedom. She need not know who comes to see him, nor why. This is a difficult lesson for many women, but one which must be learned early.

Even at the risk of one less bedroom, the clergyman must have a room in the rectory that is *absolutely* his own, one in which neither mother nor the children have free entry. This ought to be his own private haven, with a workable desk, a telephone, a comfortable chair, and plenty of space for books, as well as a sign on the door that says "Do not disturb." The entire family must respect father's right to uninterrupted hours in his study.

One of the most difficult tasks for all minister's wives is to learn to share their husbands. The doctor's wife spends many long hours alone and waiting, and so it is with the minister's wife. There will be areas in which she can never join him. Because of the very nature of his profession, he is a confidant to many, including attractive women. Words of confession that come to his ears are a sacred trust and may never be repeated. The sooner she realizes this and accepts it, the happier she will be, and the more nearly she will become the well adjusted minister's wife.

There was only one occasion when I *did* have to put my foot down. In our congregation was an old ·blind lady who had scarcely two coins to rub together. Many were the midnight telephone calls from her, just "to chat." Her landlady notified my husband that she was going to have to be evicted from her dreary one-room living quarters, because the dear soul's clothes and person were covered with lice. She could not see and was not aware of them, and unless she could find someone who was willing to put her in the bathtub the landlady would tolerate her no longer.

What would any wife's reaction be if she heard her husband say on the phone, "*I'll* come over and give Miss Murray a bath"? I was able to convince him that he was going a bit beyond the call of duty, and that if anyone was going to do the bathing and fumigating it would be his wife. An even happier solution was found, when a visiting nurse took on the job, and Miss Murray was allowed to stay in her room, appearing the following Sunday in church, cleaned-up and sanitary!

There are the lonely hours and the long waiting, and the disrupted meals. These can be weathered. Mental attitudes placed in correct proportion can be of infinite value, changing a life from the negative to the positive joy of self-giving. What satisfaction for the minister's wife when she can truly say to herself:

"Isn't it wonderful that he can be of help to people, that he is needed, that they want him? These people are God's people, and they have been placed in our care. We belong to them."

This precept that we belong not to ourselves but to God's people was brought home to us abruptly several years ago. To celebrate our tenth anniversary in a parish, recognition was made in a very tangible way, with a gift of money, large enough to enable us to plan a week's visit in Bermuda for a much needed rest. After twenty-four hours there, an urgent call reached us — one of our parishioners had met with a tragic and untimely death, and her husband wanted us back.

"Imagine being wanted that much!" "What good is a clergyman to a man if he cannot be with him in his great hour of need?" "How could we enjoy Bermuda when our hearts were back with this tragedy?"

These were some of the things we said to each other as we flew back. Then, by some miracle of the mind, the sacrifice became a privilege. The story does not end here, for our bereaved friend, out of the thankfulness of his heart, arranged a short trip to Florida for us later on.

Skies will not always be clear. There will be problems and controversies. This is inevitable. Church people are much like the little girl who had a little curl right in the middle of her forehead — when they are good, they are very, very good, and when they are bad they are horrid. What makes them horrid? More often than not, there is frustration at home, or a guilt complex, or a defense mechanism designed to cover up some deep seated problem. These are the very persons who need spiritual help. Those who are the most unlovable generally need the most loving.

For each difficult person in a parish, there are countless good Christians, dedicated souls who are eager to pour out their loving kindness upon their minister and his family in hundreds of ways. When a new baby arrives, or when sickness or sorrow comes, letters, well wishes and gifts will appear in a staggering amount. We have been overwhelmed by the outpouring of love that descends upon the minister's family in times of trouble. Unless one has experienced this, it simply cannot be imagined.

This was shown to us in a wonderful way when our two-year-old son, now a jet pilot for the Navy, was stricken with polio. A cloak of despair was spread over the congregation the following Sunday. It was not *our* son, but *theirs,* who was ill. We shall always believe that because of the prayers of so many, God chose, in some miraculous way, to spare this child of ours.

> *O Eternal God, Creator and Preserver of all mankind, Giver of all spiritual grace, the Author of everlasting life; send Thy blessing upon these Thy servants, this man and this woman, whom we bless in Thy Name; that they, living faithfully together, may surely perform and keep the vow and covenant betwixt them made (whereof this ring given and received is a token and pledge) and may ever remain in perfect love and peace together, and live according to Thy laws; through Jesus Christ our Lord. Amen.* *

* *Book of Common Prayer*

3

That Their Home May Be a Haven

Drop in any week-day morning in a large cafeteria between eight and nine, in any city, and it will be hard to find an empty table. Are all these people transients, waiting to take a plane, train or bus, as, one morning, were we? Are they bachelors who have no facilities for preparing breakfast at home? Are they elderly spinsters who eat breakfast out just for the excitement? No, they are teen-agers, high school kids, with their books stacked high under the table, grabbing a quick breakfast on the way to school.

What a shocking sight! What an indictment upon our society! Where are their homes? Their parents? Why are they not sitting around a family breakfast table, storing up not only food for energy but the spiritual and emotional strength that comes from the security of a family unit? To our forefathers the very fabric of society was built around the home, the family, the large dining room table, which is now almost impossible to purchase, and ah, yes, the family prayers are rapidly becoming a thing of the past. The divorce and juvenile courts are filled with parents who might not have been there, had they been able to bring their problems to the family council.

Somehow, someway, this trend of the decay of the home must be stopped. The rectory family has a wonderful opportunity to demonstrate what a God-centered home can be. Whether they like it or not, they do live in a goldfish bowl, and through this glass globe they can demonstrate to the world an exemplary family life — not perfect of course, but healthy and happy.

The communist countries are at least realistic about the home situation. They say at the outset, that there is nothing to this family nonsense, brushing it off as they do the existence of God. They say to their women, "Have your babies — we need more workers — we'll supply the maternity care, the hospital care and the after care — we'll pay you well to have your children — go ahead and have them — then come back to work as soon as possible."

There is a line of thinking in current books and women's magazines that does not help to preserve the sanctity of the home. They are saying to us, "Women, don't be stuffy housewives, doing your round of boring and unrewarding tasks, eating peanut butter sandwiches with your children, picking out kitchen curtains or dress patterns — you are too intelligent to waste your time on such trivia — rise up, and free yourself from this bondage, etc., etc."

So what does the housewife do? She manages to get a job with a welfare agency, a job that requires a good educational background, one that is commensurate with her capabilities. And what is her particular assignment? She interviews men, women, and children. Why are many of them in trouble? Because they have either come from broken homes, or the mother has left home to take a job. No wonder they are plagued with insecurity.

A surprisingly large percentage of clergymen's wives have been forced to take outside employment. Teaching school seems to be the most popular job for many of them, probably because of the convenience of the hours. In many cases, a second salary is necessary to keep the wolf from the door. With gratitude we note that the lay people are beginning to wake up and realize that the parson and his family cannot live on a sub-standard wage, and that his wife should not have to work to meet that standard.

"I'll never get enough of that wonderful stuff!" says the song. No matter what the salary, we can always use a little more. To the mother who tries to justify her taking a job, so that she can afford that second car, or a private education for the children, we urge her to take a second look. She may be risking her own health by burning the candle at both ends, and thus giving her best to neither her home *nor* her job. She may find that, adding up the extra expenses of a working mother, her salary may not be as large as it first seemed. Finally, the satisfaction of being with her own family, as well as with her parish family, may well outweigh the financial sacrifices that must be made.

The boring chores of the household can become pleasant experiences with a simple change of attitude or point of view. It is then, and only then, that by some wondrous change the *housewife* becomes the *homemaker*.

A story is told of a man visiting one of the quarries in England. He approached a laborer and asked what he was doing, and the answer was "Digging big chunks of stone out of the quarry." Further on, another worker seemed to be chipping the stones with his chisel. He looked at the visitor and with a gleam in his eyes said, "I am building a Cathedral."

The next time the housewife takes the vacuum cleaner to the repairman, let her take comfort from this man with a vision, and say to herself, "I am building a home."

What makes a house a home, beside a "lot of lovin' "? It is a place where mother expresses her personality and where father can slouch into his favorite chair, to relax and throw off some of the cares of the day; where the children can sense security and love, a place where they may happily bring their friends; where the good things and the sad moments of life are shared. It does not take a large bank account to make an attractive home. It is little touches that can give glamor — a few flowers to grace the dining-room table, or a carefully planned reading corner, complete with table, lamp and books.

Meals tossed at the family in haste, on the kitchen table, can become a degrading habit. Children ought to learn to live with nice things. One of my friends once told me, "We always use our best silver and china, because we're the nicest people we know." A more cynical friend used her best silver for a less justified reason — she didn't want to save it for her husband's second wife!

Each day mother is implanting ideals into the impressionable minds of her children, and memories which will mean much in the years to come. They should be happy memories — of a tidy home where the sofa is not only to be admired but to be sat upon, and where mother is not such a slave to neatness that she cannot take time out to kiss the hurt finger.

Perhaps my four-year-old son expressed his appreciation as a small child can, when he grabbed me impetuously one day after kindergarten, and said, "You're the nicest mother

and you never smell!" The homemaker is unfair to herself
if she is untidy in her attire, and wanders about the house in
hair curlers, looking like something from outer space. Recently my husband returned from a pastoral visit to a young
women, so tightly "done up" in tiny pin curlers that "she
looked like the baked ham we had for dinner last night —
with all those cloves!"

The parson's careless wife not only commits a disservice
but she courts disaster, for one never knows *who is on the
other side of that front door!*

> *O God, who has so consecrated the state of Mat-
> rimony that in it is represented the spiritual mar-
> riage betwixt Christ and His Church; look merci-
> fully upon these Thy servants, that they may love,
> honour, and cherish each other, and so live together
> in faithfulness and patience, in wisdom and true
> godliness, that their home may be a haven of bless-
> ing and of peace; through the same Jesus Christ our
> Lord, who liveth and reigneth with Thee and the
> Holy Spirit, ever, one God, world without end.
> Amen.**

* *Book of Common Prayer*

4

The Preacher's Children

Statistics tell us that more persons listed in "Who's Who" come from homes of clergymen than from any other profession.

This is small comfort to the clergyman when little Mary has just announced that she has decided not to go to Sunday school any more, and the teacher has just called to say that Johnnie has given her more trouble than any other child in the class. But statistics don't lie, and therefore we must assume that these children have learned to ride out the storm.

The interrupted meals, the frequent absence of father, the demands of the telephone and the doorbell, that at times seem so rude, the lack of privacy, and the label of being different from the other children — perhaps it is these very things that have contributed to the building of their characters. All minister's children weary of such remarks as, "We wouldn't expect this of *you*," or "What will your father think?" or "Of course *you wouldn't!*" Oh, what an invitation to a twelve-year-old — *wouldn't* he!

Our younger son, now grown, who was very "spirited" (a fancy expression for a little rascal) told me recently that every teenager has to rebel against something, as he matures, and, said he, "I had a built-in situation just made for me to rebel against — a minister's son!"

The mother of these candidates for "Who's Who" will hope that she can make their lives as normal as possible. From their earliest conscious moments they will realize that they have certain responsibilities that other children do not have. They must learn at an early age the rules of social communication, how to greet the parishioners graciously, how to take messages, how to deal with emergencies. Their actions will reflect their father, even though they may wish it were not so.

The question of church non-attendance is certain to raise its ugly head at some time. That old chestnut that Mr. Smith-was-made-to-go-to-church-when-he-was-young-so-he-vowed-he-would-never-go-when-he-was-grown leaves me totally un-sympathetic. Poor Mr. Smith! Did he give up brushing his teeth for the same reason?

Certainly there are times when we do not "feel" like going to church, but these are the very times when spiritual dis-cipline is most needed. One does not expect a child, because his father happens to be a minister of the Gospel, to have a genuine spiritual awakening at an early age. Conversion does not come about this way. To some it may come with a sudden impact, a definite moment when God speaks and says "Turn," as He did to Paul on the road to Damascus. For the great majority of souls, it is probably a gradual process of spiritual infusion and awareness. It will not harm the children to go to church when they feel rebellious. We placed the issue squarely before our children in as simple terms as this, "If you don't back up your father, who will?"

The celebration of Christmas in a rectory full of small children is a pleasant but taxing experience. The whole Christmas theme is centered around the Christ Child and the celebration of His Birth at the services of the church. The customs and traditions that have stemmed from this Great Event are a part of every home — the trimming of the tree, the hanging of stockings, and the exchange of presents.

In most families this is a time of togetherness, but not so in the rectory. Father has an early Christmas eve service, a midnight service, and on Christmas day there are services at 8, 10, and 11 A.M. Somehow, togetherness must be arranged in between services, allowing father to be present. On occasions such as this, only a sense of humor will see the family through. After our children were quite certain that Santa Claus really didn't come down the chimney, we arranged to have this mythical character make an early visit to our home the day before Christmas. Our celebration was on the afternoon of the twenty-fourth, with Christmas dinner following it.

Incidentally, this is a custom of the Scandinavian countries, so our procedure was based on sound authority. There was only one drawback to this plan. We had to remember *not* to thank Mrs. Brown for the children's toys, or Miss Mabel for the potholders, until after Christmas Day, for in the South particularly it is sheer heresy to open a Christmas present before December twenty-fifth.

I am certain that when the disadvantages and the rewards of being nurtured in a rectory are weighed, most children will respond overwhelmingly on the positive side. The contacts with all kinds of people, the thrill of sharing joys and helping to ease sorrows, the excitement of witnessing the happiness that a new baby can bring into the lives of a young couple in the parish, or the anguish felt by the rectory family when sudden death visits the home of a family in the congregation — all these and more, serve to build a character that will hold fast in the days that lie ahead.

Parishes differ from one another in spirit, and the thing that makes the difference is the dynamic spiritual commitment of its lay folk. The clergyman and his wife and children have to take a lead in making this commitment. What better than the power of example?

Many years ago, we knew an ardent, zealous woman who had become tremendously interested in one of the extremely evangelistic Christian sects. Her life was dedicated to converting other souls to her own persuasion. She met her match one day, when she tried to convert a friend of ours, who asked her this question:

"What about your husband and children?"

"Well," she admitted, "it's hard to persuade your own family."

Said my friend to her, "Well, convert them first, and then come around and I'll talk business with you."

> *O Almighty God, Creator of mankind, who only art the well-spring of life; bestow upon these Thy servants, if it be Thy will, the gift and heritage of children; and grant that they may see their children brought up in Thy faith and fear, to the honour and glory of Thy Name; through Jesus Christ, our Lord. Amen.**

---

* *Book of Common Prayer*

5

The Almighty Dollar

Jacob might have been the first man on record to "tithe" when he said, "This stone which I have set up for a pillar, shall be God's house; and of all that thou givest me, I will give the tenth to thee" (Genesis 28:22). An increasing number of church people practice the ancient rite of tithing, and they will tell you with enthusiasm that it is a way of life; that it makes the difference between giving (often through coercion) a gift *to* God and being a partner *with* God.

In the modern scheme of things, one is asked to give separately and to multitudinous causes, including the Red Cross, Community Chest, health, education, etc., etc., ad infinitum. No man has a right to tell another man how he is to spend his money, but frequently the rector is asked, "How much do you think I should give?" Many churchmen, concerned with stewardship and the matter of man's financial responsibility to his church, have suggested that 5% of one's income for the support of his church, and 5% to other worthy causes, is a fair distribution. The old adage "Give 'til it hurts" might be better expressed "Give until it feels good." But each family must work out its own system of giving, guided by the dictates of conscience, for this is a matter between a man and his Maker.

The clergyman's family will ultimately realize that the power of example is stronger than any sermon on steward-ship ever preached. A dedicated missionary clergyman in Brazil instructs his church treasurer to deduct one tenth of his salary each month and place it back into the church treasury. The result of this is that the church roster claims a large per cent of "ten percenters," and the church has grown with deep spiritual vigor, for "Where your treasure is, there will be your heart also."

The high school drop-out who learns to lay bricks well can earn a wage triple that of the teacher or the clergyman, whose training requires a high school diploma *plus* seven years of advanced study. In a conversation not too long ago with an officer of one of our large American shipping lines, I was told that the shipping company's biggest prob-lem is the one that arises from the demands of labor and wages. Imagine my amazement to learn that the sailor who swabs the deck has a larger salary than ours!

At least no one can say of the parson's wife that she mar-ried him for his money. If she really wants that mink coat, she'd better try to win it on a television quiz program, or inherit it from a rich aunt. Since the salary, in most cases, is in no way commensurate with the requirements, some mighty clever dollar-stretching will have to be performed each month. But the very stretching process can bring happy results. The homemade soup, the homemade dress, and the homemade slipcover — with these come the satisfaction of a job well done.

"I'm no good at figures," says the sweet young bride. Neither am I, but surely this is no excuse. To be a good manager of the family funds is a challenge to any woman of normal intelligence. Wall Street tells us that a major percentage of the money in this country is spent by the woman of the household, and it behooves her to spend it wisely — to see that what goes out does not exceed what comes in, and to manipulate the budget in such a way that the pattern fits the material.

Strict budget living can be very tiresome, but there ought to be some semblance of financial organization. Any stationery store can supply an inexpensive account book to help the family accountant divide the spending into such logical classifications as gifts, food, utilities, automotive, clothing, etc. Happily, in most instances, a rector's budget does not require the listing of that staggering item called "rent." A prayer of thanksgiving ought to be upon the lips of every preacher's wife each month as she ponders the good fortune of living in a rent-free home.

We have no right to pray for a sunny day for the Sunday school picnic; and the man who asks God to open an unlocked door seems to place prayer on the level of cheap sorcery; nor have we felt justified in asking God to send an extra dollar our way. But it has been our experience, more often than one can imagine, when the checking account registered zero, and all financial resources had reached a dead-end, and an urgent need arose, that the unforeseen check has arrived in the mail as if out of the blue. Then the two of us have stared at each other in wonderment, declaring in unison, "The Lord surely does provide!"

Not the least important item in the budget is that set aside for recreation — the occasional change of scenery.

Many wonderful vacation opportunities are available to the preacher and his wife, such as sponsorship of a visit to the Holy Land, or the exchange of pulpits with another clergyman at home or abroad. The minister in charge of a summer chapel has a splendid opportunity to bring his family to the mountains or seashore, in exchange for pastoral duties and Sunday services. This means "change of pulpit for him, and change of sink for her," but the very fact that it is a change will help to renew resources.

The parson who is fortunate enough to join the staff on a cruise ship is indeed a happy man. Many shipping lines take along a Protestant chaplain, offering him free passage in exchange for services. Recently this was our lot.

It has been said that the modern complicated tax structure governs a man's way of life. It influences his giving, his vacations, the way he conducts his business, and it has even given him joy at the birth of a child — not only because a new life has come into being, but with this new life comes a tax exemption. In spite of all the complaining and grumbling most citizens are willing to pay their due to their government. With thoughtful planning and careful records, computation of one's tax need not be the dreaded ordeal that the cartoonists and quips make it.

If the preacher's wife has all the financial facts at her fingertips, a great burden will be lifted from her busy husband. The greatest boon to the clergyman's household is a book entitled "Minister's Tax Guide" published annually by the editors of *Pulpit Digest*. It contains a carefully prepared, step by step plan for computing one's tax, with special examples and situations that involve the typical minister's financial set-up. Many are not aware of such allowable deductions as those for maintaining a study in the home, purchase of religious publications, the purchase and maintenance of clerical clothes, etc.

Careful records of deductible expenses throughout the year can make the task a fairly easy one. One final bit of advice, good for clergy as well as laity: Begin the job early in the year, well in advance of the April fifteenth deadline.

The importance of paying one's bills promptly and in full cannot be stressed enough. This is particularly true in a small community where the merchants will soon ascertain whether the new preacher is a good risk. The system of charging on account and paying by check is an intelligent way of purchasing goods and services, thereby making it unnecessary to carry large amounts of cash and helpful in keeping adequate records.

Charging is not for the woman who cannot afford that dress this month, for the chances are that she will not be able to afford it next month either — although I am certain that all of us, if truthful, indulge occasionally in that dream! Maybe next month won't ever come, or better yet, maybe they'll forget to send the bill!

It is extremely important to his church that the minister have a good credit rating in the community. I am reminded of the admonition of the dear head-mistress of the church school I attended many years ago: "Girls, remember that when you have on your St. Agnes School uniform everything you do or say reflects the school." The preacher's wife does indeed wear the uniform of her church in her community. If she is lax in her financial responsibilities, the merchants will soon begin to say, "Those church people don't pay their bills."

Almighty God, whose loving hand hath given us all that we possess, grant us grace that we may honour Thee with Thy substance, and remembering the account which we must one day give, may be faithful stewards of Thy bounty; through Jesus Christ, our Lord. Amen.

* *Book of Common Prayer*

* * * * 6 * * * *

The Rectory Hilton

Probably every parson's wife, at some time in her life, is convinced that she is running a first rate hotel — with one difference. The hotel has a competent staff, and at the Rectory Hilton, the lady of the house is not only the manager, but also in charge of reservations, room clerk, purchasing agent, bellboy (with an occasional lift from the male members of the household), chambermaid and dining room superintendent.

Most will agree that the added trouble involved is well worth the effort for the thrill of having so many exciting persons, from all walks of life, cross the threshold of the rectory — missionaries, bishops, seminary students, senators, college presidents, as well as ordinary folk. And any family reared in this atmosphere is richly blessed.

It means a great deal to one's guests if their likes and habits are known. Everyone ought to try out their own guest room to see that the comforts score above the minimum standard — a few suitable magazines, a booklet of personal prayers, a pin tray, a bottle of aspirin, a radio, a glass for water — it's the little things that make for comfort.

Here is an urgent plea for twin beds for the guest room. The wife of one of our bishops once gave me a blow-by-blow description of the trials and vicissitudes of the two of them sleeping in various and sundry rectories. As they grew older, like so many of us, they had found it impossible to sleep in one bed. More than once, they were proudly escorted to the best room in the house, resplendent with a great double bed. After many sleepless nights the bishop's wife devised a neat trick. She rolled an extra blanket or bed spread on the bottom sheet into a tight coil, attached to the top and the bottom at the center, and voila! they each had their own quarters.

Recently a series of Lenten preachers visited our parish, and for three successive Wednesdays we had a dietary problem. The first Wednesday came a minister on a salt-free diet, our next guest had ulcers, and the next diabetes. Although this slightly taxed the dining room department, it was well repaid by the pleasure these three delightful men of the cloth gave us.

Amongst our guests over the years, we recall with particular delight the late Reverend George Gilbert, humorist and author of *Forty Years a Country Preacher,* who laughed so convulsively at his own stories that he could scarcely finish them. He was a rare soul who had a matchless understanding of a man's true worth in the eyes of God.

Added to the list of our star-studded visiting dignitaries, was the missionary bishop and his family, who were moving their residence halfway across the globe, and arrived with eighteen pieces of luggage, requiring three separate trips to the railroad station.

One of the *un*successful ventures at our "hotel" was a surprise visit from a couple from South America, totally unknown to us. We do have some very dear friends in Brazil, he the rector of a church in Rio. A man that our friend knew *very* slightly, happened to mention that he and his wife were flying to the "States" for Christmas. On learning of this, our friends purchased a very small gift for us, and asked him if he would mail it to us from New York City. Apparently this was all the stranger needed — a likely address in the United States where they might spend the Christmas holidays. *Why mail it? We can deliver it,* this couple thought.

Imagine our surprise on Christmas eve when the two arrived at our front door, she unable to speak a word of English and he very little. "Where are you going?" we politely queried, to which came the astounding reply, "We are here!" "What are your plans for Christmas Day?" "We have none." This continued for several days, and we began to realize that they scarcely knew our friends in Rio. Four days later we decided we had contributed our share to the Christmas spirit, and urged them to be on their way, with all members of the family declaring that "Mother had been took!"

If the minister is to extend the hand of hospitality to his clerical friends, then certainly the same privilege should be given to all other members of the family. The children should feel free to invite their friends to their home, and to receive a cordial welcome.

This had always been impressed upon our children, but we were not prepared for a telephone call from our college son, telling us that one of his fraternity brothers had been selected to play lacrosse on the North team against the South, and as the game was to be played in our home city, "I told them they could all stay at our house" — "Why certainly, dear, how many?" "Nineteen!" They came, they ate, and they slumbered, in beds, couches, on the floor, everywhere except in the rafters — and all of us had a wonderful time together. And to this day our son has never ceased to express his gratitude.

Another college student came to visit us rather late in the evening. The next morning there was a hearse parked in front of the rectory. Our friend, we discovered, had purchased this vehicle at a great bargain, and was using it as a trailer to tour the country. We told him that we were happy indeed to have him, but, please, would he park his hearse down the street a way, before the rectory telephone started to ring more frequently and more frantically than usual?

That recalls another recent young visitor — a healthy fearless specimen of a Navy pilot. When he arrived at our rectory beside the cemetery, his eyes grew larger, and his knees began to quake, and he said, "Boy-o-boy, I don't think I'm going to sleep tonight near all those dead people!" Our reply was, "No problem at all if you believe in the Resurrection."

There can be no better way in the world to teach a family the spirit of brotherhood than to welcome visitors from foreign lands. Wars would be unthinkable, were the practice of people-to-people visitations carried on universally.

The Displaced Persons program, so ably directed by the Church World Service, has saved the lives of thousands of persons who fled their homeland seeking freedom. This is a contribution that has received many plaudits, but frequently overlooked is the remarkable effect upon all those American families who were willing to open their homes and hearts to these refugees.

Quite by accident, a family from Estonia, and more recently from a Displaced Persons' Camp in Germany, came to our rectory to spend a week and lived with us for eighteen happy months. Hilda, Viktor and their two-year-old girl, Tiu, gave to us more than we ever could have offered them. For from them we learned patience, industry, economy, as well as an overwhelming appreciation of our country, our way of life, and the abundance we take for granted. When they left us, we were grateful to Almighty God that we could give one small family of three a new start in life — a second chance.

Shortly after our Estonian family left us, our older boy went off to college, leaving our thirteen-year-old quite companionless. As any parson's wife knows, many evenings are spent away from home. A thirteen-year-old is too old for a baby-sitter, and too young to spend night after night alone. The solution was to find a foreign student to live with us. And that is how Yuri, also from Estonia, came to live with us.

This fine young man soon became one of us, inspiring us with his intelligence, his driving ambition, and his unbelievable tales of hardship. Having spent three years in a concentration camp, barely cheating death on many occasions, he had no knowledge of his family; he had fled his homeland on a moment's notice. When he received his degree, with high honors, Yuri left us to serve in the army of the country which had saved his life and given *him* a second chance. Yuri left an indelible impression upon all of us.

Experiences such as these should serve as a real demonstration to the lay household. Rectory families have a golden opportunity to give leadership to this sort of project.

If the rectory is ample in size, and a good many of them are, and if the family will not be overtaxed, they may be called upon to share their home occasionally with the ill or the lonely or the desperate. A most attractive woman in one of our parishes, a dear person with a very real sense of God's power, suffered a nervous breakdown. Whenever it was necessary for her husband to be away from home overnight, she was terrified to be alone. Suicidal thoughts plagued her mind. She spent several nights in our guest room, but only after the windows were securely bolted down. Poor soul, she eventually did take her own life, and that we could not do more for her has been our eternal regret.

Situations such as these may well sap the strength of the preacher's wife, and the one with wisdom and good judgment knows where and when to draw the line. It was not until I found myself nursing a sick teen-age boy from another land that it began to dawn on me that though the spirit is willing, the body cannot always keep up with that spirit.

A young lad from Bermuda was attending boarding school in this country. During the Easter holidays an operation was performed on him at Johns Hopkins Hospital. Because his uncle was a clergyman, and had known my husband many many years before, we were asked to receive him in our home from the hospital, all of which required a moderate amount of post-hospital care. This was a simple gesture of love toward a fellow clergyman, one anyone should be willing to fulfill. However, as I look back upon the incident, I realized that some cardiac difficulties were beginning to make themselves known to me, and it loomed up as a tremendous responsibility, added to the ones I already had. Of course we were only too glad to help out in an emergency, but as I fell into bed exhausted each night, it occurred to me that one must learn on occasion to know how to use that very difficult word, "No!"

O Thou who, watching over Israel neither slumbers nor sleeps, bless those who share with us this night the hospitality of our home. Comfort them in their sleep, refresh them when they awake, and send them into the new day with a grateful sense of Thy mercies, and grace to know and to do Thy will; through Jesus Christ our Lord. Amen.*

* G. A. Taylor

* * * * *7* * * * *

Contact With Missionaries

"Eat everything on your plate, dear — think of the starving Armenians." To those of us who were growing up in the second decade of this century, came this somber warning. For the life of me, I could not figure out, nor can I yet, how eating my spinach could possibly keep some Armenian child from being hungry. When the little girl drops her quarter in the Offering Box, it is possible that her young mind is confronted with the same sort of vagueness. Much as our church schools attempt in every way to motivate our young people to spread the Gospel, "giving to missions" sounds a hollow ring.

But let that same child see a real live missionary, and it is a different story. Here is reality. She listens intently as she hears him tell of another little girl in some far-off land. Her dress may be different, and the color of her skin may not be the same, but she is just the same on the *inside*. An idea is converted into a personality.

Everyone knows the crippling effect on a church when its interest and concern stays within its parish boundaries. The parish buildings may be near perfection, the equipment the very latest in efficiency, the church music may be without flaw, and the parish treasurer's balance sheet, the envy of the local merchants. But if this is it, and that is all, then it is not the church. A social club, with a set of rules to serve as guide lines, can carry on the same task, and will do it better.

The very essence of Christianity, of course, is its witness and sharing, and we are all accountable, each one of us, for carrying on the work of our Lord. The very word Gospel means "good news," and good news is for telling. A newspaper, no matter how reliable its reporting, is a nonentity unless it is read. So the story of Christianity must be circulated, lest it wither and die.

Lay and clergy alike ought to seize every possible opportunity to bring missionaries to their local parishes. Every denominational headquarters can supply a list of missionaries on furlough, or visiting this country — men and women who are eager to tell their story. Do not suppose that their sole purpose in coming is to tell the story and pass the hat. Quite the contrary. Missionaries want us to be acquainted with their work, to feel a part in it, and to pray with them for the spread of the Kingdom. "We do not want your money as much as we need your prayers," they tell us.

If the visit of a missionary to the parish is a great treat for the lay people, imagine the bonus for the clergy family, who will, in most cases, play host to these great soldiers of Christ. They will come from every field, nearby as well as far-off, domestic as well as foreign, American as well as native. For the preacher's children this will mean a built-in study course in history, geography, economics and social studies all wrapped in one — plus a great deal of fun in the bargain.

St. Luke's Hospital in Tokyo is one of the best known mission hospitals in the world, but only when its wondrous accomplishments are recounted by someone who has been there, does it come alive in our minds and hearts.

After hearing of the dreadfully crowded conditions in Japan from the wife of one of its bishops, we shall be ashamed ever to speak again of housing shortage in this country. When Mrs. Kurose tells us that, because of lack of space, her husband's diocesan office is in a little corner of their small kitchen, we learn the meaning of cramped quarters.

As Bishop Koh of Malaya spoke of the desperate hunger of his people, I recalled my recent complaint that the supermarket was temporarily out of my favorite item, and I was overcome with humility and chagrin.

The lay people in one parish have had a burning desire to help our new seminary in Puerto Rico, after hearing a member of its faculty outline the necessity for a training center for native students — natives because they can far better serve the churches of their fellow countrymen.

Ever since a full blooded Indian priest came to visit our parish and our home, the members of our family have always referred to our red-skinned neighbors as Indian Americans. The old term, American Indians, somehow seems to imply that they are not really Americans, and how well we know that they were entitled to the name long before we were!

Our love affair with Brazil began many years ago when my husband was the rector of a large parish and needed some assistance. The students of a nearby seminary were eager to get into parish work, enabling them to gain practical experience, as well as a bit of financial lift.

"I'm sorry, all of our students are spoken for," was the Dean's reply to my husband's urgent plea for help. "There is only one person available, but he would be of no possible help to you — a fine fellow — but he speaks no English. He has been given a leave of absence from his church in Brazil to take a year of graduate study here — speaks only Portuguese — Sorry."

"Send him over," was my husband's answer — an answer which he now believes was prompted by the Holy Spirit.

When the hour came for the rector to meet the train which was to bring the Rev. Curt Kleemann to us, our son intimated that it would not be hard to identify him at the station, as he would be scantily dressed, short, dark-skinned, perhaps beating a tom-tom, and very likely he would have a large ring in his nose.

We shall always remember that moment when, in the door, came a tall handsome blond, dashing and debonair, but who unquestionably bore the look of a radiant Christian. It was love at first sight for us all. As the months wore on, Curt became more and more familiar with the language. It was not long before he was able to preach — with perfect English diction, and just enough accent to add a touch of glamor. By this time he had completely won over the entire congregation, with his dedication, sincerity, humor, and his inspiring message of the Gospel.

Curt was part of the family now, so much so that we all dreaded the day that was drawing near, for Curt's return to Brazil. *Why must he go?* we thought. *If his Bishop in Brazil would loan him to us for eighteen months, why not keep him on as assistant rector? He could send for his wife Dulce, and his two-year-old daughter, Silvia. They could live with us in our spacious rectory. Think what it could do for us, and think what it would do for them.*

And so this came to pass, and the rectory began to burst its seams with joy and activity — the two clergymen working out their plans together, and the two housewives comparing notes and customs, but mainly struggling with the language barrier, for Dulce had never spoken a word of English.

This experiment in living has left an indelible mark upon us all. Our children's sights were raised, and their horizons broadened. And they, along with the other members of the parish came to realize, as never before, that the Church is not a little building on the main street of a suburb, but as large as the whole world itself.

Nor does the romance end here. After eighteen wonderful months, reluctantly, we bade farewell to the Kleemann trio. They loved us and we loved them, and a little part of us went with them.

Their parting words, "We'll see you in South America," rang in our ears for the next several years, though ever so dimly. Pray for something hard enough, and that prayer will come true. Our prayers were answered, and by good fortune, we found ourselves one day walking down the gangplank of an ocean liner, tied up in the most beautiful harbor in the world, Rio de Janeiro. There they were — Curt, a little grayer, Dulce, a little plumper, Silvia, now a young lady, her six-year-old brother Paulo. We had come to visit them for two fun-packed, emotion-filled, nostalgic weeks. A more pleasant reunion has never taken place. What we had done for them in eighteen months, they tried to do for us in fourteen days.

It was not easy for them. Their slim salary, which amounts, in American dollars, to about $75.00 a month, buys only the bare necessities. The critical inflationary state of the Brazilian economy is a cause of much concern. Many household goods, as well as many foods, are beyond their financial reach. But the Kleemanns went all out for the Taylors, and the Taylors loved it.

The high spot of the visit was at 11 o'clock on Sunday morning at Igreja do Redentor (The Church of the Redeemer). My husband was scheduled to preach with the aid of an interpreter. The church was filled, and the organist struck the opening chord. Sparks tingled through my backbone, and a lump settled in my throat as the choir proceeded down the aisle, singing to the tune of "Holy, holy, holy," its Portuguese counterpart, "Santos, santos, santos."

> *O God, Who hast made of one blood all nations of men for to dwell on the face of the whole earth, and didst send Thy Blessed Son to preach peace to them that are far off and to them that are nigh; grant that all men everywhere may seek after Thee and find Thee. Bring the nations into Thy fold, pour out Thy Spirit upon all flesh, and hasten Thy Kingdom; through the same Jesus Christ our Lord. Amen.*

* *Book of Common Prayer*

* * * * * _8_ * * * *

The Ministry of the Kitchen

Before the average preacher's wife ends her days, she will have presided over miles and miles of meals and menus. If she can learn to love it and keep her sense of humor for insulation, it will be one continuous County Fair. Her invitations will run the gamut, from hamburgers for the gang, to the most elegant of wedding receptions. In between this wide range will be the acolytes'* breakfast, the dinner for the Vestry, the supper meeting for the business women, refreshments for the afternoon meeting, Sunday night supper for the young people, as well as the cozy little dinner for six or eight and the impromptu coffee or tea party.

For twenty-five years the acolytes' breakfast on Sunday morning was a tradition in our rectory. This also included hungry curates, lonely bachelors, surprise visitors and "strays." I am certain that the pancakes that have come out of the

* In the Episcopal Church, these are the boys whom the rector uses in administering the sacraments, etc.

rectory kitchen, were they stacked, would reach the tower of the Empire State Building. We never *were* able to fill up the hollow leg that belonged to one of our curates.

Once, a pre-wedding luncheon for the bridal party of one of "our girls," had all the earmarks of success, but for one exception—the bridegroom decided not to come. Then there was the afternoon tea party, when four portly ladies packed themselves into my Victorian sofa, and came crashing to the floor, leaving the sofa in irreparable shambles, the ladies' dignity considerably damaged, and the rector's wife extremely embarrassed.

No sooner do the new minister and his wife settle into their new parish, than the invitations for dinner will start flowing. A frantic thought may come to the preacher's wife, "How can I *ever* repay all these people?" The obvious answer is, of course, that they do not expect to be repaid. They consider this an opportunity to become better acquainted with their clergy family, and this in no way puts an obligation on her.

She who entertains twenty-four or so guests from the parish — "a few of our close friends" — is treading upon dangerous soil. Twice that many will say to themselves, "I thought *we* were their close friends."

The solution to this is the Open House, given from time to time in the rectory. This automatically includes everyone in the parish, and when the sensitive touchy soul says, "They never ask *me* to their parties," the preacher's wife can always fall back on, "So sorry you weren't able to come to our Open House — perhaps next time you can make it."

Many people will find the tea party or the coffee hour is a pleasant change from the cocktail hour, so rapidly sweeping the country.

Perhaps there is no better way to know your flock than to seat two or four of them at a time around your dinner table, where tensions are relaxed, and the conversation flows freely. It will flow freely, that is, if the parson's wife has taken time and thought to be so well organized that all possible chores are completed before the guests arrive, and she can calmly greet them at the front door with a well powdered nose.

If she can give the illusion that there is a "dear little gem" in the kitchen, all well and good. I believe it is wholly possible to have a successful servantless dinner party for six or eight. With this premise one of my fellow clergy wives thoroughly disagrees. One evening in their small rectory, at an informal dinner for eight, including several VIP's, there were three servants waiting on the table, all falling all over each other. Confidentially, the cash outlay for one of them might have been put toward the food.

If the cook is to be in the parlor, she will have to plan a suitable menu. How distracting to a guest when a scintillating conversation is left in mid air while the hostess pops up and disappears. Hot little biscuits may be delicious but not if she has to leave her "participles dangling." A delectable meal, unusual in its content, arranged with an appeal to the eye as well as the taste, with a dash of watercress here, and a handful of water chestnuts there, will help the guests, no matter who they are, to enter into the spirit of the maidless meal. And we have seen more than one cold, disgruntled parishioner, who hasn't liked the way things have been going in the parish, thaw considerably over a tasty meal at the minister's house.

A cardinal rule for pleasant dining is frequently over-looked — eye appeal. A dinner may be perfectly cooked and seasoned to perfection, but if it caters to the stomach alone and not the eye, dismal failure is certain to ensue. Some time ago we attended a dinner party with a completely white menu; cream of celery soup, fricasse chicken with biscuits, mashed potatoes, creamed onions, vanilla ice cream with marshmallow sauce — ugh! I was tempted to get even with the lady, invite her back, and give her: borsch (beet soup), ham, tomatoes, red cabbage salad, and raspberry sherbet.

A well-to-do parishioner, on receiving a homemade loaf of bread as a gift, wrote to me: "If you had sent me a silver candelabra, it would not have meant as much — because you sent me a part of yourself." Few sensory satisfactions can top the aroma of bread baking in the oven (unless it is the fragrance of raspberries as they are plucked in the noonday sun). Why is it, I wonder, that more women do not tackle homemade bread? Any basic cookbook will tell them how, the main requirement being to stay home.

Once I played a game with a loaf of bread and won. The first season that we took over a summer chapel in the mountains, we drove up to the attractive cottage that was to be the summer rectory. There it was, wedged in the trees, between the road and the lake. As we turned our car around quite innocently in the road across the street, a most unpleasant woman promptly appeared to make it very clear that it was *her* driveway and she would thank us to *stay out.* Her mind was saying, "That new preacher's family needn't think they can come up here and spoil my summer — besides, I don't even go to their church." This kind of greeting we had never experienced before. Our older boy muttered "the old crab" under his breath.

As the days passed, with never so much as a good morning or hello from her, a cold, calculating decision came to me. I was going to break her down — no one should be like that forever. And so the next time I baked bread for the family an extra loaf went into the oven for our friend(?). It was delivered to her, hot and fresh. That did it! My scheme had worked, there was a miraculous turn-about. Almost weekly we brought her fresh bread, and before the end of the season, we had become good friends, we enjoyed a supper aboard her yacht, and she even attended the final church service that summer.

I have a secret weapon of good will. It is a cake mold made in the shape of a lamb. Iced with a coconut frosting, and resting on a bed of green coconut, the little lamb cake never ceases to bring delight, to old as well as young. Any simple cake recipe can be used, although one time I could have made the lamb out of plaster of paris or papier-mache. That was the time we brought one to a dear old lady recovering from a broken hip. She kept it by her bed table for months, because "I couldn't bring myself to cut into him."

The holidays offer countless opportunities for gifts from the kitchen, and if packaged in attractive and useful containers, something of the gift remains. The coffee cake, shaped like a Christmas tree or formed into the initials of a favorite parishioner is always sure to please — or the date nut bread on a decorated cutting board. Or, consider the apothecary jar filled with spiced nuts, or a wicker basket stacked with cookies. Given a little encouragement, imagination can run wild with the endless possibilities that stem from the kitchen. As the advertisement aptly says, "Nothing speaks of lovin' quite like something from the oven."

Lord of all pots and pans and things
Since I've no time to be
A saint by doing lovely things
Or watching late with Thee,
Or dreaming in the dawnlight
Or storming Heaven's gates,
Make me a saint by getting meals,
*And washing up the plates.**

* Anonymous

9

The Sympathetic Ear

The preacher's wife will hear much that can never be repeated. She must be a good listener, but never a gossip. A bishop's wife once told me that she felt like a cemetery, so many secrets were buried within her. In many cases a woman will feel freer to discuss her problems with another woman; hence, her advice and counsel is certain to be sought.

My initial opportunity as counselor came to me as a very young bride. There was an elderly spinster in our first congregation, who fancied herself a youthful miss, and dressed accordingly, with frills and bows and fancy clothes. The neighbors described her as "slightly tetched." She came to see me one day, and said she could not discuss this with "the Reverend," but what *must* she do. A certain young man (he was a fine handsome youth, recently graduated from college, and engaged to be married) stared at her every Sunday in church. In fact he made passes at her, and did I think she ought to encourage it or ignore it, for, as she said, "A girl can't be too careful these days."

This, of course, was a humorous beginning for me, and I must confess that I handled it badly, but it is not long before the preacher's wife will be called upon for some very serious advice and help. This in no way means she is to usurp her husband's prerogative. He, and he alone, is qualified to give professional spiritual counsel.

But what of the lonely woman, the shy, or even the love-lorn — conditions not quite serious enough to seek an appointment with the rector? Many there are who simply want to talk to someone who is willing to lend an ear, someone who cares. Making herself available, and appearing to have an understanding heart, the wife of the minister will be sought out, because of her very position. Here is someone who is neutral, unbiased, unprejudiced, and someone who won't tell.

Some clergymen will look upon this with great scorn. In fact, a rector once told me in no uncertain terms, "I want my wife in her home where she belongs and she is to have no part in the church life at all." The other extreme is, of course, the busy-body who wants to be in everyone's affairs, and believes that it is she and she alone who can solve most of this world's ills.

Somewhere in between are the host of minister's wives who have an instinctive compassion for human souls, accompanied by a burning desire to help them. If his wife can bind up the wounds of just one suffering soul, the rector will realize that he has a true partner in his ministry.

This is not to say that she will hang up a shingle with "Welcome, all — Advice given, free of charge." No, her type of listening will take on a far more subtle form. Her opportunities will be grasped in the ordinary give and take of social exchange — at the dinner party, the meeting, the tea, as well as the market place. Some mighty satisfactory conversations have been held in the A & P.

Even confinement in a hospital offers an opportunity for spiritual help with fellow patients. A group of us who were allowed walking privileges, gathered in the hospital room of a bed-ridden patient, each morning for meditation and prayers. A great deal of spiritual power emanated from these brief moments. It meant, too, that thought and speech were not completely dominated by operations and medications.

In a large gathering, the alert preacher's wife will seek out the woman with the troubled countenance. Unhappiness is quick to mar an otherwise handsome face. Someone just to listen may be all that is needed.

Late one winter evening many years ago in upper New York state a frantic telephone call came to me. A desperate voice said:

"You may not remember me — I met you last summer at a party — we had a wonderful talk together — I made up my mind tonight you were the one person that could help me — I am so unhappy — do you think you could come to my apartment?"

When I arrived, her large apartment, in one of the most fashionable dwellings in the city, was dark and dreary. Her husband, a prominent citizen, a "joiner" who was involved in many activities, was out for the evening. (This thought raced through my mind as I found her so alone: Here is a vicious circle — does he leave home every evening to get away from his sad frustrated wife — or is she sad and frustrated because he leaves home every evening?)

Depressed and tragic, she was in desperate need of a listener. Cooped up in her apartment, she was frightened to meet people. Her immediate worry was the thought of her son arriving home in a few days from boarding school and she wanted to be able to put up a good front. She seemed to be defeated, with nothing to fall back on.

We spoke of faith and prayer, and I assured her that I would keep her in my prayers. But at that moment, something else was needed. She must get out of that apartment. There was to be a tea in the rectory the next day for the women of the church, and I urged her to come. This invitation she declined, but said she wanted to do something to help.

"You can! How about making me some sandwiches for the party?"

Now we were on the right track. Her face was aglow, and she smiled for the first time. Why the change? Because suddenly she was *needed*. An added bonus to the incident was that the rectory never had better fare.

By the time her son arrived she seemed able to face him. But quite obviously, in this case, professional guidance was needed. It is at this point that the amateur leaves off and the professional takes over. But the ice had been broken, and the first steps had been made toward recovery.

Even partial success is not always that easy. A most attractive young woman appeared in church one Sunday. She came each week thereafter, sat in the same pew, arriving late, leaving early, and speaking to no one. Never had I seen a sadder face. It was even an effort for her to sing the hymns. Her every moment seemed impregnated with sorrow. On becoming acquainted with her, it was quite obvious that her home situation was an unhappy one. She was persuaded to come to the prayer group of some twelve young married women, at which she became a regular attendant. But she was aloof, difficult to penetrate. We could not reach her, none of us. She preferred to keep her troubles to herself, and we felt we had failed her.

This was some five years ago, and only recently I met her mother, who told me that we would never know how much the warmth of our friendship in that prayer group had carried her through a most difficult situation. She was now married, and finding such happiness as she had never before known. And her great interest in prayer groups continues.

There is no more tragic sight than the alcoholic woman. Rarely will she seek help, since one of the symptoms of the disease is an unwillingness to admit addiction. Condemnation, scolding and reprimands are not the answer. She must be treated with love and understanding, as well as an earnest effort to lead her to that superb organization, Alcoholics Anonymous.

How well I remember the lonely widow, whose life seemed so empty since the death of her husband, that she was desperate for companionship. We talked for long hours about the man she was considering for her second marriage. His unsavory background, and the record of his past performances seemed to make him a most unlikely candidate. I believe she is now grateful for having been discouraged from jumping from the frying pan into the fire.

Any mother with an understanding heart, who has children of teen age, will find the young set coming to her with their problems — generally small ones which loom up into great proportions for them. Somehow they feel rather secure in seeking advice from the minister's wife. It is the same old story. They are certain that their own parents do not understand them. To unburden their hearts to someone who will listen is all that is needed. Most of them need only to be told to go back to their parents who are ready and anxious to hear them out.

For the preacher's wife who prefers not to get mixed up in other people's lives, for good and justifiable reasons, there is another source. Why not utilize the good advice and counsel of those more experienced than she, through the use of the pamphlet? She may find it difficult to express herself, and frequently her inadequate words are better left unsaid. The professional in the pamphlet can say what she wants to say, only better.

Every rector's study should be well supplied with many of the leaflets that are now available at a minimum of cost. They run the gamut of subject matter, including "The Meaning of Prayer," "When Death Is Inevitable," "Be of Good Cheer," "On the Death of a Child." The list goes on and on. We have found them of infinite value.

". . . some should be apostles, some prophets, some evangelists, some pastors and teachers . . . for building up the body of Christ" (Ephesians 4:11), says Paul, describing the variation of talents. All of us have some special gift, be it small or great. The parson's wife may have a literary flair, or she may be interested in history, or whatever. If she uses this talent to the fullest, by sharing it with others, she will be twice blest.

Many young girls have visited our rectory with their dress pattern and yards of fabrics, and together we have worked out the plans. The main ingredient is a love for creative expression, not professional skill in sewing. And what a splendid backdrop for some heart warming discussions that will cover a world of subjects — anywhere from sewing in zippers and setting in sleeves, to the meaning of prayer and the reality of God.

This, you say, is pastoral counseling? Yes, in a sense. The skills and talents of a woman are by no means isolated from the church, for the church is concerned, and deeply so, with every phase of a woman's life — body, mind and soul.

O, Most merciful God, and Heavenly Father, Who hast taught us in Thy Holy Word that Thou does not willingly afflict or grieve the children of men; look with pity, we beseech Thee, upon the sorrows of Thy servants for whom our prayers are offered. Remember them, O Lord, in mercy; endue their souls with patience; comfort them with a sense of Thy goodness; lift up Thy countenance upon them, and give them peace; through Jesus Christ our Lord. Amen.*

* *Book of Common Prayer*

10

Her Place in the Church

Before the service, speak to yourself; during the service, speak to God; and after the service, speak to your neighbor. But what if your neighbor doesn't speak to you? There have been many tales of the cold, unfriendly church, and I like to believe these are grossly exaggerated. Anyone, however, who has been on the receiving end of the ice cube treatment knows that it does not provide an ideal climate for true worship. The church is a fellowship of believers — a *fellowship* — and without this the spark is considerably dimmed. No more important privilege befalls the preacher's wife than seeking out the stranger and extending to him the warm hand of fellowship, for, the power of the handclasp is never to be underestimated.

And during the normal exchange of greetings on a Sunday morning, she will frequently uncover pastoral information, all of which can be reported to "headquarters," where it will receive prompt attention, and action if necessary. "I was sick for three weeks and the rector never came to call" is a frequent refrain. Of course the rector does not have extra-sensory perception, and needs to be told.

When the parish plays hostess to other parishes and churches, the pastor's wife will find herself a greeter ex-officio. By instinct she will extend a welcome. Nor is this a Sunday morning affair only, but an automatic reflex which eventually becomes a built-in mechanism.

To our regret, the trend to build or buy rectories a "safe" distance from the parish grounds is a growing one, based on the argument that the family must "get away from it all." Get away from what? Having spent two years out of thirty away from the church environs, I submit that geographical distance detracts from the spiritual and emotional proximity to the House of God. Living near the church, one is aware of a kind of benediction. And certainly the shepherd can more effectively tend the pasture which is at hand.

Along with the modernization of church buildings comes the stream-lined operation of the church's work. With this has developed the establishment of ministerial office hours, which say, in effect, "You come to me — I'm too busy to come to you unless you really need me — *then* I'll come." A necessary custom, probably, since almost impossible demands are made upon today's pastor. But, oh, for a revival of the good old days, when the rector and his wife came to call, just for a friendly visit. This custom has some very sound pastoral implications, too, for if you become close to your minister in fair weather, you will turn to him more readily in the storm. Even the habit of neighbors calling upon neighbors is disappearing, along with the street car and the ferry rides. Cannot we preachers' wives revive this happy habit?

When death strikes the parish, and strike it will, what is

the role of the preacher's wife? "O Lord, give me the prudence to know when I am needed and when I am not needed, and the wisdom to know the difference." If a close friend has died, then certainly a visit with her husband is in order; but if the person is not an intimate, then the rector had better take over — unless there is something very constructive that she can do, such as care for the children, answer the door, make necessary phone calls, etc. Otherwise, it adds just one more burden to the bereaved, the burden of being sociable.

I recall a particularly pathetic phone call from a dear elderly gentleman. "Is your husband there — No? — Well, I think my wife is dead on the couch — she was taking a nap, but she won't wake up — yes, I've called the doctor."

While the secretary attempted to locate my husband, I drove out to his home to see what help was needed. The woman had indeed died, and the stricken man was there alone with the long-time devoted maid bewailing the loss of her mistress. "While your son is making the three-hour journey, what can I do?" I asked. Whereupon the stunned, but well controlled gentleman found his Christmas card list, and said, "Please call all of these people and tell them about Bessie." Always I shall remember the emotionally exhausting task of broadcasting that sad news for three consecutive hours. But with a grateful heart there was the realization that the Lord had placed me in this situation at the correct moment. This I believe.

The shut-ins, the lonely, those recuperating, the newcomer to the community, these will always respond with joy to a visit from the minister's wife, for she is attempting to bring something of the church to them. If she also brings a small sample from her kitchen, all the better.

Hospital calls, however, are definitely to be avoided, except by the clergyman himself. Ask any member of a hospital staff, and they will tell you that patients recover in spite of visitors. When our first child arrived, it seemed as though all twelve hundred members of the congregation wanted to see the rector's first-born, and kill his wife off in the bargain. People came to visit me in the hospital whom I had never seen before and have never seen since. Psychologists may have the answer to this extraordinary phenomenon. But one lesson was thoroughly learned from that experience: if the "no visitors" sign is not on the hospital room door, it ought to be.

Let the parson's wife ponder diligently before she accepts an office in a parish organization. A bishop's wife admonished: "Spread yourself thin all over." It is likely that the preacher's wife may be more skilled at presiding over a woman's organization than any other member of the congregation. But by doing so she may be denying others. The encouragement of lay leadership has, more than once, been responsible for a shy member of the congregation finding herself president of a woman's group in the church — never having known her own hidden potential.

Some good friends of ours undertook the charge of a small mission in a downtown area with some twenty-five or thirty members. After seven years of hard work on the part of the minister and his capable wife, the parish grew to sizeable proportions. It grew while he wore out many pairs of shoes, and she took on the Sunday school, the Altar Guild, the Choir and the women's work single-handed. Between the two of them, they accomplished a seemingly impossible task in the name of our Lord. They have left this parish, and time alone will tell whether her strong leadership left them ready to carry on in the same wonderful way, or whether they will suffer from sudden lack of leadership.

Taking on the work of the church on a larger level is a different story. Most boards of this nature list a smattering of clergymen's wives upon their rosters. The advantage works both ways. The experience she brings from her own parish can contribute much. Even more important is what it does for her. She begins to see the church as something far greater than the tiny parochial cell she represents. I know this to be true, having presided for several years over a Diocesan woman's organization. In this capacity I was called upon to speak and counsel with almost every parish in the large Diocese, an experience certain to widen the narrowest mind.

In every town and hamlet there is a minister's wife who has learned the hard way; how to stand on her feet, how to speak to a large gathering, yes, even how to expound the Gospel on occasion. It is fitting that these talents be put to good use. Who amongst us has not shared my fright when called upon for the first time to say grace publicly? All that came to mind on this occasion was my telephone number!

With the exception of the mother of young children, or the working wife, or the woman in poor health, the minister's wife should be eager and willing to enter into the full life of the parish. Her talents will greatly differ. One wife with a love of music, will sing in the choir. Another with teaching ability will help out in the Sunday school. Still another will have a flair for flower arranging for the altar, and so on. But talent or no talent, all of us can offer our home for an occasional meeting. The rectory belongs to the congregation. Why not let them share its comforts? If there are *discomforts* let them share these, too.

It's surprising what happens. At a summer seaside parish, the ladies were invited to the summer rectory for the annual women's meeting. The living room furniture, with its squeaky backs and uncomfortable seats, had been there since the beginning of time. Perhaps Providence seated the president and most influential member of the Guild on the lumpiest chair. By the end of the summer, some changes had been made. A somewhat unorthodox way to get new furniture!

Almighty and everlasting God, Who dost govern all things in heaven and earth; mercifully hear the supplication of us Thy servants, and grant unto this parish all things that are needful for its spiritual welfare. Strengthen and confirm the fearful; visit and relieve the sick; turn and soften the wicked; rouse the careless; recover the fallen; restore the penitent, remove all hindrances to the advancement of Thy truth; bring all to be of one heart and one mind within the fold of Thy Holy Church; to the honour and glory of Thy name; through Jesus Christ our Lord. Amen. *

* Forward Movement: *Prayers New and Old*

11

Her Place in the Community

The Ecumenical Movement will succeed only if it is promoted at the grass roots level, in every hamlet, town and city, where Christian people gather for worship. A Japanese student said, "Don't talk to us of love. You Christians send many divided religions to us and you do not even love one another." Every opportunity ought to be seized upon to bring the various denominations together in their worship as well as in other Christian endeavors. A great superstructure of an organization at the top with many branches is not the answer to Christian unity. It must commence at the bottom with the Methodists, Presbyterians, Baptists, Lutherans, Episcopalians, etc., working and worshiping side by side.

Every clergyman's wife has a chance to serve as her church's ambassador to such gatherings as the World Day of Prayer or Lenten Union Services. It is high time that we put away our petty bickerings — and time, too, that we begin working toward the vision of the One Great Church of

Christendom. For a house divided against itself cannot stand.

Any community offers a marvelous arena for the clergyman's wife who wishes to offer her services beyond her own parochial sphere. Board memberships, health clinics and fund drives are only a few of the many avenues of service.

Most new mothers are terrified of their brand-new slippery, squirmy infants. By the time my babies arrived, I was an old hand at it, because I was fortunate enough to have served in a baby clinic where my particular assignment was to take temperatures, weigh, and prepare the infants for the doctor.

Nor would I have learned the art of basket weaving, had I not served in the Occupational Therapy Department of a large hospital, teaching the patients many skills, which helped to fill the lonely hours of a bed-ridden existence.

I learned something of mass production, too, when I undertook a sewing class of some illiterate, poverty-stricken housewives in a slum area of the city. Experiences such as these reveal the fact that no matter how dedicated the volunteer service, when it comes to benefits, the volunteer herself usually comes out the winner.

There is nothing quite as satisfying as a job well done. The empty pockets of a clergyman may speak eloquently of his inability to finance a part-time secretary for a welfare agency. But he can go one step better—he can send his wife.

If one's church happens to be in a college town, there will be many events that will bring together "town and gown," such as concerts, lectures, athletic events. Any city offers all sorts of cultural exhibits and opportunities. Even the smallest town will gather its talents from time to time, to offer a community venture, such as a fair or a strawberry festival. It is right and proper that the minister and his family enter into the life of the community to the fullest—saying, in effect, "the church is supporting these efforts."

O God, Who didst plan the Gospel for an un-divided Church; refuse not, because of the misun-derstanding of its message which rends the unity of Christendom, to continue Thy saving work in the broken order of our making. Prosper the labors of all Churches bearing the name of Christ and striv-ing to further righteousness and faith in Him. Help us to place the truth above our conception of it, and joyfully to recognize the presence of the Holy Spirit wherever He may choose to dwell among men; through Jesus Christ our Lord. Amen.*

* Forward Movement: *Prayers New and Old*

*   *   *   *   *12*   *   *   *   *

Her Devotional Life

When a friend returned from a freighter trip half way around the world, I asked her how she occupied her time for those four long months at sea. "I knitted the ribbon dress I am wearing and I read the Bible from cover to cover." Most church people have read much of the Bible at some time or another ("I skip over all those 'begats,'" they say). But until one has tried the experiment of reading it from beginning to end, as one might read *Gone With the Wind* or *War and Peace*, the Bible's impact cannot be imagined. The drama of God's purpose and revelation tops even Shakespeare.

This doesn't mean that the Bible cannot be read to advantage in many other ways. The historian will read it with his own emphasis, while the novelist, the dramatist, the comedian, the lawyer, the psychologist, and the little child will each find something in it for them. It can be read by topics, by chapters, by verses, as biography, or as a travelogue, following the journeys of St. Paul.

Sitting beside me at a large dinner party was a college professor, a self-styled agnostic, who thought he'd try me out. "What do you think of St. Paul? Don't you think he was a dreadfully pompous bore?" Theological arguments are not my forte, but by good fortune I had that very morning read the seventh chapter of Romans. I attempted to defend the gentleman from Tarsus by saying that he himself did the very things he did not want to do, and did *not* do the things he wanted to do — "You call that pompous?"

The Bible contains God's promises, His warnings, His words of love and comfort. Its sacred pages permit us to share the rich and glorious spiritual experiences of men like Abraham, David, Peter and Paul. We read our Bibles to learn God's will for us, to receive His assurance in times of sorrow and peril, and to find direction for our lives.

Let no one imagine that it is strange and unnatural to pray. The contrary is much closer to the facts. It is far more unnatural *not* to pray. We instinctively reach out for something higher and greater than ourselves. Man's search for God is universal and eternal.

Prayer is entreaty, aspiration, resignation, consolation and inspiration — all of these things and much more, too. Prayer is natural, yet also alien. Prayer is familiar, yet incredibly strange, simple yet formidable.

"Many otherwise reasonable people," says Bishop Wilson, "seem to think of prayer as something to be taken up or set aside at one's convenience. There is nothing," he continues, "more pathetic than the self-sufficient person who has paid little or no attention to God, but who suddenly finds himself confronted with a desperate situation and flings himself on his knees in a frantic appeal to the throne of Grace. His soul is numb from disuse. He is a stranger in God's presence. He cries, he moans, he cringes, he roars and wonders why

the comforting relaxation of trust in God's mercy is so difficult to attain. He is like an untrained craftsman trying to
handle a delicate instrument. When we least feel the need
of prayer, that is the time when we should develop our ability
to pray."

God is made known to us in many different ways. Sunday
after Sunday, in places the world over, the corporate worship
of the church is kept alive. The faith of the worshiping
congregation lifts us to heights we can scarcely hope to attain alone.

The communion service is perhaps the most rewarding,
concrete and tangible method of receiving Grace. It is here
that the Source of Power awaits us through Christ's own
Gift of Himself.

In recent years there has been a tremendous growth in
little prayer fellowships all over the world. They are to be
found in the most unexpected places, including the United
Nations, The United States Senate, and an empty railroad
car in Grand Central Station. Group prayer is in the great
tradition of the church, instituted by our Lord Himself. A
prayer group plays an extremely important role in the life
of any parish.

The private devotional life of the clergyman's wife is perhaps most important of all, for it is here that she finds
strength, inspiration, guidance and courage to live her life
as God wants her to live it. No one can tell another how to
pray or what to pray for. However, a plan for daily devotions ought to include several orderly steps just as there are
definite plans and materials that go into the construction of
a building, or ingredients which make up a recipe.

First, she must set aside a certain regular time each day
for her private prayer life — a time and place of complete
solitude. This will require strict discipline, especially for

the busy mother of growing children. A short period of silence should begin her devotional period, giving her an opportunity to surrender her doubts and sins and shortcomings — a housecleaning of her soul, so that God may enter in.

Next comes a reading from the Scriptures. There are any number of pamphlets and suggestions for this, or perhaps a verse or chapter of her own choosing will best suit her needs. "Search the Scriptures for in them ye have eternal life" (John 5:39).

After God has made Himself known to her through His Word, let her pour out her soul to Him in her thanksgivings and her prayers of intercession and petition. God is a personal God and wants and expects us to come to Him in prayer, even as a child would come to her own father.

Now that the minister's wife has spoken to Him, let her keep silent and wait, in order that He may speak to her. "Be still and know that I am God" (Psalm 46:10).

From this quiet time of waiting will come definite response. She may see how she herself can help to bring about the answers to her earlier prayers of petition. "Faith by itself if it hath no works is dead" (James 2:17).

God spoke to me very clearly one day to bring this point home. A neighbor across the street was suffering from a cancerous arm which had grown to a monstrous size and was a repelling sight. Each day she was in my most ardent prayers — "Ah, yes, you pray for her — why don't you go to see her? That's what she really needs — she is lonely." Of course, I had been so selfish that my prayers for her had been empty and meaningless. From this experience I learned that our private devotional life is of true value only if there is a definite action and commitment that follows.

The minister's wife can read any number of books about prayer — how, when, why, where — but when all is said and done there is only one way to learn to pray — that is, to *pray*. This she must do with sincerity, conviction, and faith, for these are the indispensable qualities for the preacher's wife. And she will find that they can be both stimulated and sublimated in prayers.

Life will not always be serene. There will be some mighty rough spots in the road. There may even be times when she wonders why in the world she said "yes" to that clergyman so many years ago. To her, we say, take comfort in those wonderful words from St. Paul's letters to the Romans, that "all things work together for good to them that love God" (Romans 8:28).

> *I will try this day to live a simple, sincere and serene life, repelling promptly every thought of discontent, anxiety, discouragement, impurity, self-seeking; cultivating cheerfulness, magnanimity, charity and the habit of holy silence; exercising economy in expenditure, generosity in giving, carefulness in conversation, diligence in appointed service, fidelity to every trust, and a childlike faith in God.*
>
> *In particular I will try to be faithful in those habits of prayer, work, study, physical exercise, eating and sleeping, which I believe the Holy Spirit has shown me to be right. Amen.**

* Forward Movement: *Prayers New and Old*

* * * * * *13* * * * *

Experimenting With Small Groups

This country is experiencing a great resurgence of church attendance, and for this the Christian cannot but be grateful. Many theologians, nevertheless, look upon this trend with some suspicion, wondering if church-going is concomitant with spiritual growth. They point out that, with all the revised interest in church, and in spite of the many new church buildings and parish houses that have appeared on the horizon, the rate of crime continues to be on the increase.

The pews are filled with good Christian folk, who live decent, worthy lives, governed by moral ethical principles. Read over the membership list of the Board of Trustees of the Community fund, or the Red Cross, or the YWCA, or any other charitable institution. By and large, these men and women, the cream of the crop, will have strong church affiliations. This is not coincidence. Into their work-a-day world they carry their religious life.

Were the majority of these good persons questioned about

their beliefs, and what motivates their lives, their answers would be vague. Honesty would force them to admit not only to a lack of knowledge of the Christian faith, but to a lack of possession of one as well. These upright, devout, faithful Christians take their places in church at 11 o'clock on Sunday, and at 12 o'clock they pull down the shades of their soul, not to be raised again until the following Sunday. And if it happens to rain, or Aunt Nellie comes for her annual visit, or if Saturday night was especially demanding, well, then they may not show up until a few weeks later.

Something is missing. Spiritual hunger is a serious malady. But like the Chinese lad who, on his inadequate diet of rice, has been in a constant state of physical hunger for so long that he was not aware of it, even so countless Christians are not aware of this hunger within their souls. While obesity remains our prime health concern in this country, our souls remain undernourished.

Congregational worship can be an inspiring experience. In our present parish, the service of worship is broadcast over the air one Sunday each month for the benefit of the shut-ins, the hospitalized, and those unable to attend church. A friend of ours who had listened in, remarked that it doesn't seem the same; something is missing, he insisted. Of course there is. A worshiping fellowship can kindle a fire, impossible to transmit over the radio. The power of the Holy Spirit can lift a praying congregation to great heights. We reach a pinnacle, but oh, so soon are we back in the valley again.

What, the ordinary churchgoer wonders, do I know about the great prophets that foretold the coming of the Messiah, or about the miracles of Jesus, or of those who witnessed to His Divine Leadership? Who is this God to whom we pray each Sunday? Is He really a personal God? How can I make Him mine? Soul-searching questions, these.

"I wish some of us could get together occasionally, to try to learn more about what we believe, and how to make effective use of prayer," a woman said to me one day. Not long after that a young mother confessed to me, "I wouldn't admit this to another soul — in fact, I'm embarrassed to tell *you* — but I really don't know how to say my prayers." When still a third woman told me that she had an utter lack of knowledge of the Bible, and wanted to do something about it, I found myself being led to a decision. This was to gather together a group of fellow Christians for the purpose of study and prayer. It was as if a Voice was needling me, "Go on — I *dare* you!"

To me this seemed to be a logical area into which a preacher's wife might step. *With the full blessing and encouragement of the rector*, we decided to give it a try. Great leadership qualities are not necessary, a degree in theology is not required, nor is a scholarly interpretation of the Bible essential, else few prayer groups would have ever been started. All that is needed is an instigator with courage and determination.

In our large suburban parish, many little groups of workers gathered together to prepare for the Annual Bazaar in the Fall. One summer a group of a dozen women, many of whom were my personal closest friends, met each week at the home of the chairman, to make cookies. Cookies, cookies and more cookies. These were packaged attractively, and frozen to be ready for use at the Fall event. I proposed to them a plan: "We're good friends — we work together — we play together — how about being serious together? Suppose we come an hour earlier for meditation, study and prayer, before we begin our work?" No one wants to be put on the spot, to be unwittingly drawn into something not of their own choosing. "Don't come at 10 next week unless you really think it's a good idea — skeptics stay home — otherwise you will hinder its purpose — don't tell me now what you think of the idea — go home and think about it and pray about it — come at 10 if you want to — otherwise, we'll see you at the cookie-bee."

There were 12 there that day. The following week 14 appeared at 10 o'clock. And there began a great spiritual force within the parish. What tremendous power has been released from this group since that day of its inception. Many years have passed, and this small gathering still meets regularly in that upper room, broadening the horizons of each member such as she has never dreamed.

Another group in the parish met each Wednesday during the summer, to sew. They had a wonderfully gay time, laughing and working, with time out for a box luncheon. That the parish house was the coolest place in town was an added inducement. At noon they entered the chapel for prayers and intercessions. As I think back now, the Lord must have smiled at the assorted multicolored scraps that were pinned to their heads, as substitutes for the traditional hats.

These few hushed moments seemed to be the high point of the day. When their sewing was completed, and their meetings came to a close at the end of the summer, I suggested that we had had such a pleasant time meeting together, why not continue meeting for an hour each week for study and prayer? It has been my experience that the word "Prayer Group" frightens some away. "Study Group" may be preferred. After all, what's in a name?

They were told to think about it, pray about it, and come the following week at the appointed time, only if they were interested. This proposal was made to a dozen, and the next week 18 appeared. This group, too, has been meeting on and off ever since.

Soon the leaven was beginning to work within the parish. Several more small groups came into being, an overflow from the sewing group (more than 18 becomes too large). A gathering in the evening for the working women, a young married couples' group, and an early morning gathering for young mothers materialized.

Sufficiently encouraged, we called together a number of socially prominent friends, some of whom rarely attended church. The same proposal was suggested to them, and they backed the plan 100%. Recently on a return visit to the parish, I met one of the women from this group. She came up to greet me, her eyes filled, and looking straight at me, said, "You changed the whole course of my life."

What do you do at a study group or a prayer group? There are, of course, as many answers as there are groups. The hour should include Scripture reading, meditation, discussion, and prayers.

Prayers will be offered for those in need, sickness, sorrow, as well as thanksgivings. However, the great ministry of intercession must not be overlooked. Any prayer group that is vibrant and alive today will want to intercede for such vital concerns as better race relations, the unity of Christendom, and a world at peace. Members of any group, whose intercessions include such scope, will come to realize what their responsibilities are in bringing about these goals.

Prayer groups have been compared to harness makers and to channel diggers. Some groups, though perhaps unwittingly, come to believe that God is in harness, waiting only for the tug of the reins to do the driver's bidding. For such there is but dismal failure, since prayer is anything but a one-way street.

In contrast, the channel digger works against the elements of nature — water, tide and weather. After a series of successes and failures, two bodies of water become joined, and there is a two-way communication flowing freely between the two.

I believe that the very heart and soul of a well knit prayer group is this: Each member is asked to remember each other, by name, individually, in her daily time of prayer. At first it may be the mere mention of the name. As the weeks go on, however, a great fellowship of prayer develops, which can only be imagined or described by those who have experienced it.

> *Almighty God, Who has given us grace at this time with one accord to make our common supplications unto Thee; and dost promise that when two or three are gathered together in Thy Name Thou wilt grant their requests; fulfill now, O Lord, the desires and petitions of Thy servants, as may be most expedient for them; granting us in this world knowledge of Thy truth, and in the world to come life everlasting. Amen.**

* *Book of Common Prayer*

* * * * *14* * * * *

It Is More Difficult to Receive Than to Give

Don't tell me that doctors are primarily concerned with the almighty dollar, that surgeons bleed the public, or that the medical profession is a mercenary one. Such complaints will fall upon deaf ears. I shall come to their defense to my dying day, which would have been long before this, had I not reaped the benefits of their mercy.

It is a well-known fact that doctors give free service to the indigent, but not as well known is their courtesy service to the clergyman and his family. Our babies were not only little gifts from Heaven, but little gifts from the obstetrician. He was a very dear friend of ours, this man who *gave* us our children. Some twenty-five years later, in a very small but sorrowful way, my husband was able to compensate, by ministering to Dr. Tom Gamble as he lay dying of cancer, helping him to accept death as a Pathway to Life, and comforting his courageous wife.

The custom of free medical care is not always easy to accept gracefully, although once in my husband's early ministry it backfired. Having arrived at his first new large parish with a severe cold, he glanced over the parish list and selected one of the doctors at random, who promptly and courteously gave him medical care and banished his malady. In seminary days, he had heard tales of doctors "taking care" of the clergy. A month passed, and receiving no bill he selected the most appropriate gift his money could buy, and delivered it with a card expressing his gratitude. Already in the mail was the bill which he received the following morning!

Every preacher's wife will agree that it is difficult to express to the doctor the real gratitude that is in her heart. The medical viewpoint was made eloquently clear to me, however, by a man I am bound to classify as "just a little lower than the angels." Shortly after we had come to a large suburban parish, one of our small boys contracted scarlet fever, and promptly transmitted it to me.

A doctor, not a member of our parish, had been recommended to us, and he came to the rectory immediately. I remember saying to him, "Now let's get this straight — you are going to have to make daily visits here for a while, plying us with penicillin, etc. — you are not a member of this parish — I would like to feel free to call upon you — won't you make it a strictly business proposition and send us a bill?"

He looked at me and said, "Now I want *you* to get *this* straight — I would never have been able to enter the medical profession without the kindness and goodwill of many people — your husband spends his life helping others, helping the sick, picking up where we leave off — this is what I can do for him — so it's a closed book and don't ever mention it again!" I never did, but the good doctor did not realize that he was bargaining for a very large order. Ten years later when a serious illness felled me, he called at the rectory almost every single day for two months and every other day for three months more — and *all for the love of it!* My indebtedness to him, even now, sweeps over me in a wave of my own unworthiness.

This is only a sample of the reasons for my personal gratitude to the medical profession. With deepest humility, I must bear witness that, through surgery, the gift of life was given to me by one of the outstanding surgeons in the country — and I mean quite literally *given* to me. However can one say "Thank you"? An unwanted, expensive, useless gift which will end up in a rummage sale is certainly not the answer. I am told that doctors have attics filled with useless gifts from gp's (grateful patients).

The minister can only hope to express his gratitude in prayerful thanks to these angels of mercy. There is no denying that the Holy Spirit is never more apparent than when He is seen working through the talents and skills of the doctor.

In our little country parish, quite near the church, I had a magic oak tree. One Sunday morning a visitor noticed me placing two empty egg boxes at its base. Her expression of curiosity seemed to require an explanation. This was my magic tree, I confided to her, and it laid eggs instead of acorns. What's more, it laid them neatly in egg boxes. And sure enough, after the service there they were. All this because one of the dearest ladies alive kept the rector's family supplied with eggs, and she and I found the tree a handy exchange mart on Sunday mornings. This is only one instance of the outpouring of love that never ceases in a rectory household. Our freezer is stocked with wild game and the fruits of the field, and our larder with pickles and preserves.

This is in no sense vainglory, but merely a statement of fact. Just as the grace of God is freely given, not earned and often not deserved — so God's people choose to express their love for their church, by bestowing gifts upon the shepherd of the flock.

Holidays, tragedies, illnesses are an open invitation for flowers, food and gifts that are showered upon the parson's family in unbelievable abundance. Only once did the shower turn into a devastating torrential storm. When it was discovered that confinement to my room for a six-month rest had been ordered by the doctor, many problems were created. Who would answer the telephone, listen for the door bell, run the household, make the beds, do the laundry, plan the meals? With all of these we were somehow able to cope.

The rector's biggest problem? Returning the plates and bowls and dishes that arrived daily with food enough to supply the neighborhood. Each morning my husband re-received his briefing: "Mrs. Brown's wine jelly came in *this* bowl, Mary's chicken on *this* platter, the fruit salad on the glass plate from that nice Miss Smith — the pewter dish belongs to Betty, the glass one to Miss Mabel — don't forget that the basket goes to the Joneses, and Dorothy wants her cookie tin returned, etc., etc., etc." The rector gained ten pounds and I was on a diet.

Nor are these wondrous expressions of love for the church confined to food alone. They often consist of thoughtful little gestures that would seem to be activated by the Holy Spirit.

A friend of mine, whose husband is now a bishop, told me

of her delightful experience. For two weeks they were to be in Miami officially at the church's convention. A woman in the parish who had just returned from a year's trip around the world, called at the rectory one day and said, "It was necessary for me to have an unusually large wardrobe, one for all seasons and all occasions — you and I are the same size — would you be insulted if I offered to lend you my wardrobe?" My friend most gratefully accepted the kindness, and her husband tells me that she felt like Cinderella at the ball.

The list goes on — tickets to the opera, the symphony orchestra, the baseball game, or the occasional check seemingly out of the blue. When we moved into a new rectory, was it necessary to obtain the services of a professional mover? No indeed! Pick-up trucks arrived from all the neighboring farms, and the job was completed with dispatch and fervor. What is more, the windows were shiny bright because the busiest career woman in the parish spent two of her precious off-days washing them.

To express adequately one's appreciation is not easy. And the sense of unworthiness and humility is in no way alleviated by our Lord's words to Peter when He said, "Everyone to whom much is given, of him will much be required" (Luke 12:48).

> *O God of Love, we yield Thee thanks for whatsoever Thou hast given us richly to enjoy, for health and vigor, for the love and care of home, for joys of friendship, and for every good gift of happiness and strength.*
>
> *We praise Thee for all Thy servants who by their example and encouragement have helped us on our way, and for every vision of Thyself which Thou*

hast ever given us in sacrament or prayer; and we
humbly beseech Thee that all these Thy benefits
we may use in Thy service and to the glory of Thy
Holy Name; through Jesus Christ our Lord. Amen.*

* Forward Movement: *Prayers New and Old*

＊　＊　＊　＊　*15*　＊　＊　＊　＊

Sorrow, Need, Sickness, or
Any Other Adversity

Let no one suppose that the clergyman's family is freer
from the vicissitudes of this life than any other family. In
spite of all the jokes about it, the preacher has no hot wire
communications with God, nor does he receive, or expect to
receive, preferential treatment from the Almighty. He is
subject to all the ills and anxieties that his flock have.

Although much of the sickness of this world is brought
on by the misuse of one's body, or by ignoring the laws of
science, nevertheless the accident, the unearned sorrow, and
the just plain hard experiences cannot be explained away.

We hear a great deal today about the relationship between
sickness and sin. God, we are assured, wills for us health,
or wholeness of body, mind, and soul. Even though the healing Christ said, "Thy faith hath made thee whole," still there
can be danger when one man, be he clergyman, spiritual
healer, or whoever, stands in judgment upon another. A fine
young mother in our parish, a devout Christian, awoke one

morning to find her child stricken with a mysterious incurable malady. She attended a meeting at which a clergyman spoke on spiritual healing. He convinced that earnest,
loving mother that some guilt of hers brought on the child's
illness. She became so depressed that she herself became
emotionally ill.

What a negative approach that speaker had taken. Our
concern should be not so much with *why* we are visited
with affliction, but *how* we bear it.

"He is such a good person. Why did this happen to him?"
Just because he is good in no way insures a man against hard
times. The saint and the sinner are shown no discrimination.
"He makes the sun to rise on the evil and on the good, and
sends rain on the just and on the unjust" (Matthew 5:45).

Knocks and bruises are good for us. They help to build
character, changing our foundations from shale to rock.
We know that the Lord does not "willingly afflict the children of men," but we are aware, too, that these very afflic-
tions may be used constructively. The other day, a close
friend, returning home from the hospital, with a cast on her
broken knee, said, "This is the first rest I have ever had in
my life — I'm sure there was a purpose in this accident." As
she said it, a radiance was upon her face that I had never
seen there before.

A short time ago a young boy named Everett Knowles
made medical history, when his arm, which had been completely severed from an accident, was attached, and after
many operations and ordeals, had miraculously become a
useful limb once again. His doctor, who noticed the wonderful change in his personality, has been quoted as saying,
"Having his arm ripped off and put back on may be the
best thing that ever happened to him." Whereas before he
was listless and dull, he now has an interest in his future —

a yen for education, and purpose in life. "Why, he's actually motivated," said a hospital therapist.

What a perfect chance for the clergy family to demonstrate to their congregation the Christian's behavior and bearing of sorrow, need, sickness, or any other adversity. The preacher can expound from the pulpit forever about the acceptance of affliction. Only the deed will prove his sincerity. The doctor, unable to give up the habit of smoking, admonishes his patient, with a twinkle in his eye, "Do as I say, but not as I do," knowing full well that he is unconvincing.

Illness is bound to visit the parson's house at some time or another. Just how the family reacts will have a great impact upon their congregation. What a golden opportunity to preach a living sermon.

Suffering from the intense pains of bursitis, my husband declared, in between "oohs" and "ahs," "Now I know I'll be more sympathetic to the fellow who's in pain. From now on, no one can ever tell me that pain isn't real."

One of the most memorable Sundays in my life came as I sat in my usual pew one Sunday morning, listening to the rector preaching one of his best sermons on prayer and God's healing power. He closed with this sentence, "And now I am going to ask each one of you to offer prayers for my good wife who enters the hospital tomorrow for heart surgery."

At that moment I realized that there was no turning back. My confidence in the doctors and surgeons was absolute, and a blanket of calm spread over me as a Voice seemed to say, "I won't let you down."

But as I lay looking at the ceiling of that hospital room, the night before the operation, fear did indeed raise its ugly head. Once I had read in the newspaper about a young boy who was sent to the hospital the evening before a tonsillectomy. Late that night he found his clothes, dressed in the dark, and somehow sneaked home without detection. I knew exactly how he felt as I glanced longingly at my clothes locker.

What is my Faith, I thought. If it is just a code or a philosophy or a set of rules, it won't be of any help to me now when I most need it. I suddenly became aware of the nearness of God, and the companionship of Jesus Christ. By holding His hand, I knew that I could go through any ordeal, no matter how terrifying.

Cards were sent to every woman in the parish, stating the exact hour of the operation. They literally poured out their strength in my behalf. As a result, I became uplifted to heights that I had never known. I felt their love working through faith and prayer.

For the next three days, as life and death played nip and tuck, it would be dishonest to say that my hand remained tightly gripped to the Hand of God. Frequently, that grip was broken, and I seemed to descend into Sheol (as the Psalmist puts it), the dreary dark place of nothingness. I know now that my Faith was insufficient, and faltered. In spite of all this, He chose to spare me. I quote from a letter from my doctor: "Obviously, it was pleasing to the Lord that you should regain your state of well-being. He must have further work for you to do."

The will to live is a tremendous force in the world. We had a blacktop road in front of our rectory, and once in a while a few tender blades of grass pierced through that hard surface to reach for life, with power that seemed insurmountable.

After a long recuperation, we knew that life would be very different for this preacher's wife. No more would be the busy active existence, when physical strength was not even questioned. It was to be a newer and perhaps a fuller life, quiet, calm and meditative.

Energy in one's system can be compared to money in the bank. Checks are drawn on the account, according to the amount that is there. She who overdraws that account is in for trouble. First things must come first, and the little unnecessary foolish expenses must be foregone.

As I offer daily thanks for the gift of life, I am mindful of the brave and saintly souls who have been far more courageous than I, and yet have lost the battle of life.

A fine couple moved into our community a few years ago. He had decided to retire early while there was yet time to enjoy life. His dream house had been on the drawing board for years, and now it was to become a reality. With only a minimum of professional help, he fashioned it with his own hands. The two of them entered into the life of the parish, endearing themselves to all who knew them. One day, as she and I were sewing, she said, "Our house is almost completed now — one thing worries me — when there is nothing more to be done on it, I wonder what Walter will do with himself — he likes to be busy — and he most surely will become restless."

Not long after that, a severe pain sent him to the hospital for tests and observation. Results? Diagnosis, cancer. Walter had said to the medical authorities, "Give it to me straight — how long will I live?" And he was told the somber facts. His wife, equally brave, donned her nurse's uniform that had been stored away for many years. Together for the next few months they faced their task, with controlled emotions, with never a thought of self-pity, and a resolute faith in God. As the inevitable death came, the entire congregation was inspired by a glorious acceptance.

In a case very similar, and in the same year, a man in the

prime of his life heard the word "leukemia" from his doctor — the dread disease that is, as yet, incurable. This fine man, with the help of his devoted and devout wife, faced up to reality. He asked for the blessing of Confirmation, something that he had put off for many years. He reviewed his worldly goods, and attempted to teach his wife the rudiments of his real estate business in the remaining few weeks. She was constantly at his side, reading him the Psalms and other passages from the Bible, as his pains and fears intensified. When the end came, her spirit and resignation was a sermon to us all.

This sort of thing, of course, is being repeated all over the world. These two saintly women are only a sample. But when the day of crisis arrives for the minister's wife, she will find no better pattern than the one so carefully and prayerfully drawn by these two courageous souls.

> . . . *And to all Thy people give Thy heavenly grace; and especially to this congregation here present, that with meek heart and due reverence, they may hear and receive Thy Holy Word, truly serving Thee all the days of their life. And we most humbly beseech Thee of Thy goodness, O Lord, to comfort all those who, in this transitory life, are in trouble, sorrow, need, sickness, or any other adversity . . . . Amen.* *

* *Book of Common Prayer*

* * * * *16* * * * *

All Work and No Play Make for Dullness

Man is an instinctively gregarious creature. An experiment conducted recently by NASA, in which young Wilden Breen was locked up into complete isolation for five months, bears this out. As he stepped from his lonely, windowless, soundproof chamber, he was quoted as saying, "I've decided I like people."

Social contact and exchange of words and thoughts between human beings is as important to them as the food they eat. Any psychologist will tell us that at the moment when communication ceases between a man and his wife, there is trouble ahead.

One of the strongest arguments against celibacy is that a man is in need of a mate, with whom he can talk over the events of the day and discuss his problems, and to whom he can unburden his soul. He *must* turn to someone. Most wives, and more especially the minister's wife, have experienced this routine: 2 o'clock in the morning — he has a weighty problem — restless — can't sleep — wakes her — talks over the matter with her — then falls asleep — while she takes on the problem — lies awake. After all, what are wives *for?*

But where is *her* sounding board? To keep her life in proper balance she will most certainly need an intimate friend or two — a companion, a confidante, a first-name pal who accepts her for herself alone. One day at a meeting of the Rectory Club (an organization of clergy wives) there was an interesting discussion of this subject. To my startled ears one member expounded in detail her theory that the clergyman's wife should not be very friendly with anyone in the parish, and that she should not allow anyone to call her by her first name.

As I left the meeting that afternoon, this young woman was very much in my heart and prayers. I could not erase from my mind the image of a self-imposed cold and lonely life in which there was no one to turn to in times of joy and sorrow. Only ten days later, the city was rocked by the news that her husband, a much loved and respected minister, had ended his own life. With a hurried visit to her that day came the realization that she, and she alone, with her Creator, would have to weather this tragedy.

Friendship, like love, is not a cold, calculated process, nor can it survive the severe scrutiny of analysis. True, there may be common interests or similar backgrounds, but there is another more important indescribable element that can best be likened to an unseen electric wire that in some way establishes a rapport between two persons. You can like a person, respect her, admire her, want to emulate her, but when you "click" with her that is something again. The preacher's wife ought to have at least one "clicker."

To slough off the worries of the day and to forget temporarily its pressing needs, there is nothing quite so refreshing as a compelling, absorbing hobby. The range is unlimited and the field wide open.

There are the active hobbies, such as bowling, golf, or gardening, and the passive ones of reading and writing. There are the social hobbies of club memberships and the solo hobby of the collector. Playing golf for the pleasure of the game is one way to release tensions; on the other hand, a hobby with a useful end result may be another's "cup of tea." In the latter category, sewing is highly recommended. It not only satisfies the creative urge, but has the added dividend of a useful product.

A trick I learned many years ago, when the children were small, came to my rescue more than once. When the inevitable measles, chicken-pox, and mumps came to our house, the prospect of weeks of confinement held no dread for me. A sewing machine, a pattern, and a few yards of fabric, alternating with the thermometer, the rubbing alcohol and the bottle of pills kept mother from a severe case of cabin fever.

Sometimes a totally selfish spree, even such as a steam cabinet and massage treatment, may give a woman a much needed lift — this from personal testimony. Or there may come a day when she has a compelling desire to *do* something for someone else, finding satisfaction in the very doing.

The longest day in my life might have been even longer had I not made use of a hobby of mine. Thoughts raced through my mind something like this: "My little two-year-old — in the hospital — the doctor thinks it's polio — it will be four hours before the final tests give us the answers — must do something — can't just sit here and pray — must do something — something for someone else — yes, that will be the best therapy possible." And so I spent those terrifying hours baking sugar buns for the neighbors. For me, it saved the day, and I was able to accept the bad news when it finally came.

But, alas, I had not reckoned on one thing — the neighbors were *terrified* of me, let alone the products from my kitchen. How thoughtless had I been. Of *course* they didn't want their children to get polio. I was the "Typhoid Mary" of the neighborhood and they wouldn't even let me in the door!

The creative hobby of art or music has a soothing effect that no tranquilizer can ever give. The important factor is that it requires complete absorption. By thus ridding herself of any festering inhibitions, the minister's wife may avert a visit to the psychiatrist's office.

Whatever a minister's wife does, there should be occasions when she does exactly as she wishes, with no feeling of accountability to the parishioners.

*O Divine Master of our days, Sanctify our friendships, guide us in our pleasures, and in our free time pursuits, lead us to things beneficial for ourselves and for others. In Thy Name we pray Thee. Amen.**

* G. A. Taylor

17

Laughter Is the Best Medicine

"There is a time to weep, a time to laugh," and may the good Lord protect the preacher's wife who cannot laugh, for great will be the weeping. In the realm of nature, the ability to laugh is reserved for humans only. Not a guffaw nor even a titter will come from the rollicking colts in the field or the kitten chasing its tail, even though they may be having great fun. A sense of humor comes only with the ability to understand and communicate.

What is laughter? A difficult emotion to explain, for what may seem humorous to one is not so to another. It can give a lift to a person's soul, but it can be very cruel indeed when humor is at the expense of someone else. A tough little neighbor dropped into our house one day, and we were laughing heartily at a story he was relating. He stopped, cocked his head and said, "Hey, are you laughing *at* me or *with* me?" When assured we were on his side he continued.

There is Sarah's laughter of unbelief, the sneering laughter of the cynic, and the coarse laugh of the practical joker. There is the silent laughter of the clown, and the spontaneous laugh of the child. There is the artificial laughter of the woman who didn't get the punch line, and the hearty laughter of the wit. Laughter can soothe and laughter can hurt. It takes courage to laugh at one's own self. And only the person who perceives the little comedies within the drama of everyday living will enjoy life to the fullest.

In the solemnity of the worship of the church, a humorous situation occurs, which is funny simply because it *does* happen in church.

Any parent knows the power of the small child to make the unconscious blunder. My children were fascinated by a character called Mr. Peanut, who walked the downtown streets, costumed to resemble a huge peanut, handing out roasted nuts to passersby. Now it happened that every spring the children from each parish in the diocese made a pilgrimage to the cathedral to present their children's lenten offerings for missions. The first time I took my small son, he was spellbound by the long colorful procession of clergy, many choirs, and other dignitaries. At the end of the procession was the bishop, resplendent in his golden cope and mitre. To my horror my child yelled out for all to hear, "Mommy, here comes the Peanut Man!"

A smile still parts our lips as we think of the elderly curate who suffered immensely from the hot weather. During the summer months he wore his cassock over his underwear — no trousers. His secret was concealed until he made a reverent bow at the Altar. He was very reverent from the knees up but bare legs are *not* reverent. He had an even more embarrassing experience on another hot Sunday morning. Having prepared the holy table for the communion service, he stepped to the side of the altar to turn on the fan. At this point the communion wafers took off into the air like a flock of sparrows!

A lady fainted, once, during the sermon. It was a moment of anxiety, of course, but in retrospect it had its humorous side. A new curate completely forgot his dignity, and must have thought he was at a boxing match. The sermon still going on, he walked from the altar, down the middle aisle, stood up in the seat of the back pew and yelled, so loudly that he almost recalled the lady from her faint: "Is there a doctor in the house?" The rector preached the same sermon the following Sunday and no one recognized it.

My husband and I have laughed and laughed over the lay reader who read from Holy Scriptures about the Ethiopian "unch." And a ripple of smiles swept through the congregation as the Bishop, at Confirmation, laid his hands upon the bald head of the newel post of the altar rail.

Many humorous events have taken place during the years of pastoral visits. The rector was calling one day on a wonderfully courageous woman in the parish who had been blind for many years. During the course of the conversation, she rested her head in her hand, and rubbed her glass eye with her finger. Suddenly the eye popped out like a ping pong ball, and rolled across the rug. "May I trouble you for my eye?" said the lady, never once losing her composure. Her caller took his clean handkerchief to retrieve the lost eye, returned it to the owner and nothing more was said.

Perhaps the most embarrassing experience of the rector's life happened one summer when he decided to call upon a fellow clergyman's wife, whose husband had left home to become a Navy chaplain. We had heard that she was finding it difficult to make the adjustment, and he hoped he could be of some help to her.

Their cottage was near the lake, and the children were

swimming. Asking for their mother, he was told she was not home (a little white lie suggested by mother who wished to see no one!). My husband went into the kitchen to leave a note on the kitchen table. *This is an attractive cottage,* thought he. *I wonder what the rest of it is like.* He wandered into the living room, the dining room, and finally the bedroom. There he came face to face with the lady of the cottage, huddled behind the crude closet curtains because of her state of undress! He said "Excuse me!" and ran. On his way home he wondered what appropriate remark he could have made. The next time it happens he is going to say, "Where is the fire? — I thought I smelled smoke!"

Give me a good digestion, Lord,
And also something to digest;
Give me a healthy body, Lord,
With sense to keep it at its best.

Give me a mind that is not bored,
That does not whimper, whine or sigh;
Don't let me worry overmuch
About the fussy thing called I.

Give me a sense of humour, Lord,
Give me the grace to see a joke,
To get some happiness from life
And pass it on to other folk.*

---

* Anonymous: from a tablet in Chester Cathedral, England

18

Call to a New Parish

Soon after the preacher's wife is settled into her first rectory, she will become aware of a certain transiency of parish life. New opportunities and calls to other parishes will come to her husband, and inevitably, decisions must be made.

Divine guidance most certainly plays a part in the destiny of its clergy. Even so, some are known to circumvent Providence, and still others feel that occasionally the Holy Spirit needs a bit of nudging.

All decisions of staying in a parish or of moving to a new one, should be completely in the hands of the minister himself. Many angles will be involved, and of course he will discuss it thoroughly with his wife, but her wishes can only be secondary. Her duty to accept his final decision is absolute. What the minister looks for in a parish may present a far different picture from that seen by his wife.

He wonders, will this be the opportunity where I can best serve the Lord, will there be a challenge, will these people be responsive to my message, will my talents and abilities bear fruit here? In short, is this where God wants me?

Because she is human and feminine, and very much of this world, her secret questions will run something like this — what is the rectory like, the facilities, the kitchen, how many bedrooms are there, and is there a good school for the children? No matter how satisfactorily or unsatisfactorily these questions are answered, she knows, deep in her heart, that these superficial concerns are not really the important ones. The challenge of her husband takes first place, and if she does not face up to this truth, some unhappy days lie ahead.

Army and Navy wives know all too well the difficulties of moving from place to place. Stakes can be buried mighty deep over a period of years, and the uprooting, especially when there are children, is emotionally disturbing.

First of all, the housekeeping mechanics of a move create problems. When we had been in our first parish for a dozen years or so, circumstances seemed to indicate that a move was inevitable. I looked at the curtains, so shabby and tired looking, and wondered, "Shall I or shall I not? Shall I make new ones, and do some refurnishing and some redecorating, or shall I wait and see?" For a few more years we managed to "make do." Finally, unable to bear the old curtains any longer, I made some beautiful new ones, at considerable cost. The day they were finally hung was the day that my husband decided to accept a call to a new parish.

A minor crisis such as this is soon a humorous memory, as the anticipation looms up of a new home, new color schemes, new friends. Along come thoughts of new goals and new ideas. As the attic is emptied of its worn articles, of use no more, one's mind seems to be relieved of some old worn-out ideas, too. With the sorting of a twelve-year accumulation of material possessions come memories fond and otherwise — that old suit that father wore to the White House one memorable day, the first lock of golden hair, the painting of the reindeer that Aunt Gertie gave us. The list goes on and on, as the parade of the past marches by.

When the parade is over, its place is taken by thoughts of the future, and the new challenge to be met. We promise ourselves we won't make the same mistakes. We have a new chance.

How can we ever bid farewell to those whom we have come to love so well? The task is made less difficult, knowing that for everyone we leave there is another ahead — not to replace, but to add to the long list of dear friends. The problems we leave behind us, too. But we fool ourselves if we believe there will be no more. They are certain to be there — probably larger and weightier. The farthest fields are always greener, and we are thrilled by the challenge of a new world.

There are clergymen and clergymen — all sorts and conditions. They are no better and no worse than the laymen, because, of course, they come from the laymen — not as some suppose, from a special little set of do-gooders. Their talents and their tempers vary. If only congregations would realize that the perfect minister does not exist, a good many heartaches might be spared.

A parish church we knew very well, took well over a year to find "just the right man" for their rector, during which time it never occurred to them that they were anything but the "right parish." A selection was finally made, but only after someone sized up the situation thus, "They're looking for a combination of God and Clark Gable."

The new rector may be an especially good preacher, or

an understanding and faithful pastor. He may have administrative qualities, or perhaps he is a money raiser. All of these talents, or some of them, will come in handy. But there is something far more important than any of these. Every committee interviewing a prospective new pastor, should ask him to roll up his trouser legs. Let them inspect his knees. If there are callouses on those knees, they have the right man.

There are the "long stayers" and the "quick movers," with advantages to each. Pastorates of 15 years or more duraation bring with them a bond that securely links the pastor with the life of his people. He has the great privilege of presenting a young lad for Confirmation, watching over him as he suffers and recovers from a serious illness, presiding over his marriage, and baptizing his babies. At times he feels as if he has his finger on the heartbeat of the world, as he sees the older generation leave us, one by one, for the Higher Life, and a new generation taking its place.

There is the other side of the coin, however. Should a rector remain too long in the same parish, especially when he has won his way into the hearts of his people, there comes a tendency to worship the man himself. Unwittingly, he may stand in the way of true worship.

Those clergymen who prefer to stay no longer than four years or so with the same congregation may find that they can do a more effective job. Yet to the "long stayer" it seems a short span of time to really dig in and belong.

Just as there are all sorts and conditions of clergymen, so, too, the types of parishes run the whole gamut, from the smallest country parish, to the large city church, with its busy parochial program. Parishes, too, seem to take on a color and a flavor. Frequently, because of the geographical locale, they have a predominance of certain types — teachers, laborers, foreign-born, students, or whatever else. Blessed is the parish that has a cross-section of life within its confines.

In Episcopal Church circles, the old chestnut of "high, low, and middle-of-the-road" never ceases to be bandied about. A man speaks of a "high" parish, or a rector who is "middle-of-the-road," and the chances are he would have a difficult time trying to explain what he means. "High and crazy, low and lazy, broad and hazy," seems to sum it up fairly well. The important factor is that a minister be God's man for the particular church he is serving.

Some laymen labor under the impression that the method of finding a new rector is much like that carried on in the personnel office of an industrial firm. Quite the contrary. Different, too, is the custom of other churches. The Roman Catholic priest is appointed by his Bishop, while the Methodist is placed, and frequently moved, by the Conference. The rector of the Episcopal Church is selected by the vestry of the parish, with the approval of the Bishop. His rectorship is, more or less, for good, unless he chooses to leave. When there is a vacancy in a parish, and the clergyman would like very much to be considered, he must rely upon his Bishop, his friends and associates to place his name for consideration — a system far from perfect.

There follows the game of "cat and mouse." He must not be too eager, lest he be disappointed when he does not receive the call. Likewise, the parish "plays it cool," for they somehow do not want to suffer the seeming insult of being turned down.

A prospective candidate is frequently looked over by members of a vacant parish, of a Sunday morning. If they can manage it without the poor unsuspecting prospective knowing it, so much the better.

Two so-called "spies" invaded our parish one Sunday to size up the rector. It was a large parish, and they sat in separate pews, confident that they would remain undetected. It just happened, however, that we had been tipped off, so I found myself in the role of "counter spy." One of the men took his seat in the rear of the church, on the side, directly under a stained glass window depicting the story of Nicodemus. By coincidence, the rector preached about Nicodemus that Sunday, and unknowingly, suggested that the members turn around to see the Nicodemus window. There was the "spy," looking like the cat that swallowed the canary. We were called to that parish, where many happy years were spent. There were countless laughs, too, as Dr. Kloman, the "spy," never failed to tell his famous Nicodemus story.

We hear of the misfits and unhappy relationships between pastor and people, but by and large, and in most instances, a wonderful love-bond is cemented between the two.

The church in a small town was looking for a new minister and they had invited a series of visitors, prospective candidates, to preach in the church each Sunday. The first week, the parson, arriving a little early, stopped at the corner drug store for a cup of coffee. While chatting with the owner across the counter, he said, "What do you know about this church? What kind of people are in the congregation?"

"What kind of people do you have in your own congregation?"

"Oh, they're gossipy and difficult, and not very warm or friendly."

"Same kind of people here," was the druggist's reply.

The following Sunday, another parson dropped by, and asked the same question, "What kind of people are they?"

"What kind of people do you have in your own congregation?"

"The most wonderful people in the world," replied the parson enthusiastically.

"They're the same here," said the wise druggist.

Most gracious Father, the Giver of all good and perfect gifts, who of Thy wise providence hast appointed divers Orders in Thy Church, give Thy grace, we beseech Thee, to Thy servant to whom the charge of this congregation is now committed; and so replenish him with the truth of Thy doctrine, and endue him with the innocency of life, that he may faithfully serve Thee to the Glory of Thy great Name, and the benefit of Thy Holy Church; through Jesus Christ our only Mediator and Redeemer. Amen.*

---

* *Book of Common Prayer*

19

Sunset Years

In our church yard stands a mighty oak tree, estimated to be several centuries old. With her age-worn bark, and her limbs mis-shapen into arthritic snarls, she dominates the scene. Each year little saplings spring up from the ground around, but most of them are annihilated with the first storm. Few possess the sturdiness to withstand the rigors of the elements. As in the jungle, the survival of the fittest is the rule of nature.

This mighty oak seems to preach a lesson to me each time I gaze at her grandeur. It is this — that with the aging process comes a deep sense of security. A raccoon makes his home in a large hole high up in a limb of the old oak tree, the squirrels steal her acorns, the winds try to blow her down, and even humans drive great nails into her trunk to secure the electric wires. But there she stands, impervious to harassments from the outside.

Why is it that we humans fight age, the most natural process in the world? Of course it behooves a woman to present a pleasing and neat appearance, but why, O why, does she feel she must try to stop the clock? Millions of dollars are spent each year by women who want to look and stay young, unmindful that maturity, as in the oak tree, has a beauty all its own.

This maturity does not come simply from aging or growing old. It results from victory over life's bumps and jolts and knocks. Little does the preacher's wife, or her husband, know of the struggles that lie ahead, as they set out upon their life together. Arriving in their first parish, they are filled with hopes and dreams. Still ringing in their ears are the words spoken by his relatives, and hers, "That man will be a bishop some day." He recalls, too, the admonition from his own Bishop, on the day of his Ordination:

"We have good hope that — ye have clearly determined — to give yourself wholly to this office — will apply yourself wholly to this one thing and draw all your cares and studies this way — that ye will continually pray to God, the Father, for heavenly assistance — that by daily reading and weighing the Scriptures, ye may wax riper and stronger in your ministry — that ye may so endeavor — to sanctify the life of you and yours, and to fashion them after the Rule and Doctrine of Christ, that ye may be a wholesome and godly example and pattern for the people to follow." (*Book of Common Prayer:* Service of Ordination)

Sobering thoughts, these. Together they set out to abide by them, with earnest prayer, good hard work, and devotion to the cause.

But alas, the honeymoon is soon over, and they run slam bang into a parochial crisis. This is inevitable, for no parish is immune. Dealing in personalities is a delicate game at best, and in the church it is magnified. Why? Because God does not call upon His ministers to be "men pleasers," but to bring his flock into the knowledge of God. More than once he will stand alone in his decisions against wrong. Even at the risk of a furor, he must stand on what he believes to be right.

The well-meaning but misguided layman, who steps out of line, must be made to realize that his ways are not always God's ways. We do not like to hear the bald truth about ourselves from the pulpit; we prefer to be lulled into a sanctimonious state of self praise. But this is not God's way. And because God's way is not the easy way, there is certain to be controversy from time to time.

Conflict comes from another source too — from the minister himself. Every man is entitled to a few honest mistakes, and this does not rule out the clergyman.

In the beginning, lacking know-how, he is bound to make mistakes. It may be a serious or costly one. Perhaps he takes upon himself such powers as are assigned by law to the Vestry, thus stirring up a justifiable storm. While the young minister might let the situation get out of hand, the older and experienced man, on realizing his error, is more apt to get to the root of the problem, ask forgiveness, and nip it in the bud.

Unfortunately, many conflicts within a congregation stem from some trite, casual remark or unwitting act that begins with a tiny spark, and if not quickly snuffed out, becomes a conflagration. It can begin as simply as this: The rector publishes a list of women who served on a committee of a successful parish project. He wished to thank them publicly — but, oh my, he left Mrs. Jones's name off the list quite by accident. Mrs. Jones says it was no accident. She remembers sounding off to the rector one day because he did not ask *Mr.* Jones to usher on a certain Sunday. Mrs. Jones says the rector was getting even with her, by omitting her name.

Silly? Of course, but it can happen. Mrs. Jones enlists a few of her disgruntled friends, they line up like the Philistines, and the battle is on.

The poor inexperienced minister did not learn in the seminary how to handle a situation like this, and he suddenly finds his church a battlefield. They call him on the phone, taking up his time with malicious gossip.

And the minister's wife? They give vent to their anger by ignoring her on the street. If it is unpleasant for him, it is agony for her. No blade can cut deeper than criticism of her husband. Her heart cries out to defend him publicly. But this is only for the inexperienced. Over the years she will learn to be silent, willing to listen, but not to comment. She must go about her business just as if nothing had ever happened. Little by little she forms a hard shell around herself, like the turtle, where she may hide until the storm is over. We have found that the very best way to deal with cantankerous souls is to heed the admonition of St. Luke: "Love your enemies, do good to those who hate you, pray for those who abuse you" (Luke 6:28). It works. We know it does, because we have tried it.

The early years of the ministry, which bring enthusiasms as well as disappointments, so soon pass into history. And the preacher and his wife approach a new era. With the middle years come a great peace and satisfaction. Problems no more seem insurmountable. Home life takes on a change, since children have flown from the nest. New adjustments must be made. With the sadness of this departure come compensations. The house stays clean, the food bill drops, and the silence fairly shouts. Gone are the days of baby-sitters, measles, and teen-age late hours.

There is time now for the rector and his wife to call on the faithful together, and to receive callers. There is a new communion that was never possible before — a singleness of purpose, too, that comes from a long life together. A romance of many years, which has ripened into a deep and abiding understanding can demonstrate to a parish the meaning of a steadfast love between man and wife. Recently, a friend told us, to our delight, that we were the best possible advertisement for marriage.

With the satisfactions, there are, nevertheless, temptations. There is the temptation to lose enthusiasm for new ideas, saying, "We've tried that before — it will never work"; the temptation to neglect the daily appointment with God, in study, meditation and prayer; the temptation to become lackadaisical, giving in to the inevitable aches and pains; the temptation to grow mentally lazy — we are told that the firefly only shines when it is on the wing; so it is with the soul and mind — when we rest them too much they become inert and darken.

There comes the final stage in the life of the clergyman and his wife — retirement, which is possible at 65, and perhaps mandatory at 70. Time was when retirement meant simply an old man in a vacuum. The late Bishop Oldham used to tell of a recently retired gentleman who was asked by a friend what he did all day.

"Well, I get out of bed in the morning, open the front door to get the morning paper, look through the obituary column, and if my name is not there I go back to bed."

Thankfully, this is no more. Current phraseology bestows upon them the title of senior citizens, and they are very much a part of modern life. With some careful planning ahead, and some real mental adjustments, the final years can be extremely happy ones. Busy ones, too, for in most places there is much work available for the spare parson. Like the oak tree, he and his wife will be weathered by time, and there may be slight impairment of health, but he is a free lancer now. He can preach the Word of God, administer the Holy Communion, and call on the sick. The administrative headaches are no more. Those are for someone else now. Together, he and his wife are free to visit around the Diocese, helping out in divers capacities. If they are in reasonably good health, and have acquired an absorbing hobby or special interest, it is quite likely that they are the happiest couple around.

They know that life is not going to go on forever. Separation is inevitable. However, because their lives have been built, little by little, on a firm foundation, and they are totally committed to the will of God, there is no dread nor fear.

Although it was many years ago, I still recall most vividly a sermon on immortality preached by an eighty-year-old minister, the late Rev. Dr. C. Sturgis Ball. A smile of serenity swept over his face as he said:

"For years I have dreamed of coming face to face with my God. I look forward to death as a most exciting venture."

Abide with me; fast falls the eventide;
The darkness deepens; Lord, with me abide:
When other helpers fail and comforts flee,
Help of the helpless, O abide with me.

Hold Thou Thy cross before my closing eyes:
Shine through the gloom and point me to the skies;
Heav'n's morning breaks; and earth's vain shadows flee;
*In life, in death, O Lord, abide with me.**

---

* *The Hymnal of the Protestant Episcopal Church:* No. 467